MADE-TO-MEASURE PROBLEM-SOLVING

MADE-TO-MEASURE
PROBLEM-SOLVING

❖

Victor Newman

Gower

First published 1995 in hardback
by Gower Publishing

This paperback edition
published 1997 by
Gower Publishing
Gower House
Croft Road
Aldershot
Hampshire GU11 3HR
England

Gower
Old Post Road
Brookfield
Vermont 05036
USA

Victor Newman has asserted his right under the Copyright, Designs and Patents Act 1988 to be identified as the author of this work.

British Library Cataloguing in Publication Data

Newman , Victor
    Problem Solving for Results
    I. Title
    658.403

    ISBN 0–566–07566–0

Library of Congress Cataloging-in-Publication Data

Newman, Victor.
    Problem solving for results/Victor Newman.
        p.   cm.
    Includes bibliographical references and index.
    ISBN 0–566–07566–0
    1. Problem solving.   2. Management.   I. Title.
HD30.29.N48   1995   94–44973
658.4´03–dc20   CIP

Typeset in Garamond by Raven Typesetters, Chester and printed
in Great Britain by Biddles Ltd, Guildford

CONTENTS

❖

PART IV   SOME CONCLUSIONS

LIST OF FIGURES

PREFACE

With so much written about creativity and problem-solving, many managers find themselves confused as to which technique or approach to use, and when they should be deployed.

The purpose of this book is to introduce you to a problem-solving process map enabling you to locate and select specific techniques when solving problems.

There is a danger in sticking to the same techniques, and in not taking the opportunity to experiment or develop new techniques.

> You should not have a favourite weapon, to become over-familiar with one weapon is as much a fault as not knowing it sufficiently well.
>
> Miyamoto Musashi, *A Book of Five Rings*

My intention is not to overload you with techniques, but to provide you with the choices and the opportunity to plan your use of these techniques to develop the best solutions, while developing your own repertoire.

Victor Newman

ACKNOWLEDGEMENTS

❖

This is usually the part of the book that only your colleagues and friends worry about. I should like to thank the people who gave me the freedom to think and to play: Peter Sackett at Cranfield, Richard Killick and Penny Cox of Coopers & Lybrand, and all the clients who dared and still dare to let me loose in their businesses.

VN

PART I

HOW TO USE THIS BOOK

❖

1

YOUR PROBLEM-SOLVING STYLES PROFILE

❖

To gain best value from this book you need to complete the Problem-Solving Styles Profile (PSSP) below. Do this now.

THE PROBLEM-SOLVING STYLES PROFILE (PSSP)

This profile is designed to give you some initial insight into your own problem-solving styles. Experience has armed you with ways of doing things which work for you. This profile is part of a process of understanding your own areas of strength and may provide a focus for discussing areas for development.

This profile should take no longer than 10 minutes to complete. Your honesty will determine the usefulness of the exercise. There are no right or wrong answers. Answer on the basis of what you actually do, as opposed to what you try or would like to do.

For each of the statements listed, if you feel you would do it put a tick (√) by it. If you disagree more than you agree, put a cross (x) by it. Mark all statements with either a tick or cross.

1 ☐ I prefer to stand back from the problem and view it from all perspectives.

2 ☐ I carry out planning in two stages: I determine the key steps and then I look at the detail required.

3 ☐ I like to develop a wide field of alternative solutions before making a choice.

4 ☐ I feel that a study of the relative power of forces within a situation is key to knowing where change can best be made.

5 ☐ I don't believe in adopting the first idea which comes into my head.

6 ☐ I believe that the way to gain consensus and commitment is through inviting participants to fine-tune the original plan.

7 ☐ I like to consider all the available options, comparing them against each other.

8 ☐ I tend to work on the basis of existing tried and tested solutions, making minor modifications.

9 ☐ Time spent explaining and restating the problem at the beginning of a meeting to work on it, is never wasted.

10 ☐ I feel it is better to do something quickly than spend too much time thinking about it.

11 ☐ In gathering data, I collect not only that which supports my preferred picture of a problem but also the data which seems to offer contradictions.

12 ☐ I think it is dangerous to consider too many alternatives.

13 ☐ I prefer to have a range of practical alternatives before deciding upon a solution.

14 ☐ I am willing to step back from a situation to capture all the data to focus on the real problem.

15 ☐ I always encourage everyone to display and explain all their ideas in their own words.

16 ☐ I always anticipate the high level of detailed thinking which may be necessary to deliver a course of action.

17 ☐ I prefer to talk through all aspects of a plan with others to ensure that no areas are omitted before taking any action.

18 ☐ I don't get irritated with people who talk to little purpose.

19 ☐ In solving a problem, I draw up criteria for a solution which can then act as a filter for my wilder ideas.

20 ☐ A plan is just a piece of paper until it has been subjected to a disciplined review.

21 ☐ I feel that in order to be accurate, my work must be detailed.

22 ☐ It is not just the weight of the relevant data, but our ability to discern any trends or messages within it that is important.

23 ☐ I won't let a project progress without planning to understand all the data available.

24 ☐ I like to know how what I contribute as an individual, and what we (as a team) jointly contribute, will combine to deliver the final goal.

25 ☐ If you dive into the situation, you can always modify your approach as you begin to understand more about the problem.

26 ☐ In project-planning, I schedule a creative phase, and plan the best way to manage it.

27 ☐ I prefer to make a decision based upon clear, logical choice.

28 ☐ I like to sift out all the problems which cumulatively affect my decisions.

29 ☐ I will not support a vague general commitment to action.

30 ☐ I believe that it is vital to produce a clear statement of the problem.

31 ☐ I tend to sit back and review the individual factors and relationships which have determined a situation.

32 ☐ I listen to what other people think before forming my own conclusions.

33 ☐ When I'm working on a serious issue, the more I learn about the problem, the more the problem itself seems to change.

34 ☐ I prefer to get on with things rather than spend a lot of time thinking about them.

35 ☐ I think it is best to work with a wide range of ideas, because it is more likely that the best one will emerge.

36 ☐ I tend to ignore pressure to accept the obvious solution.

37 ☐ I do not like to undertake a task when the objectives are not clearly specified.

38 ☐ I feel that it pays to visualize the solution as a stream of activities which, together, deliver the solution.

39 ☐ My attitude is to think things through clearly, before taking action.

40 ☐ I check everyone's understanding of their own contribution to the solution.

HOW TO USE THE PROFILE

Mark off those question numbers which you crossed, in the eight-stage profile frame below.

In stages 1–7 below, a crossed question indicates a possible area for development. Two highlighted questions suggest a potential training need.

In stage 8, the situation is *reversed*. A single un-crossed box indicates a possible area for development; two uncrossed boxes suggest a potential training need.

You should now have some idea of where the opportunities are for developing your own problem-solving style within the eight stages. This knowledge will help you to plan your reading and application of the techniques.

You will find all eight sections in Part III: The Problem-Solving Process.

FIGURE 1.1   THE PROBLEM-SOLVING PROFILE FRAME

Stage 1: Identify problem

9	18	30	33	37

Stage 5: Select solution

7	13	19	27	36

Stage 2: Gather data

11	14	21	23	32

Stage 6: Plan

2	16	29	38	39

Stage 3: Analysis data

1	4	22	28	31

Stage 7: Test/Rehearse

6	17	20	24	40

Stage 4: Generate solutions

3	5	15	26	35

Stage 8: Action

8	10	12	25	34

2

THE PROBLEM-SOLVING PROCESS WHEEL

❖

The contents of this book are integrated through the Problem-Solving Process (PSP) wheel. Your completion of the Problem-Solving Style Profile should indicate opportunities to develop your own problem-solving style, and help you to plan your reading and application of the techniques.

The PSP wheel breaks down our problem-solving activities into eight defined areas, much like a map. These eight areas provide reference points to manage our problem-solving journey. By using the PSP wheel to manage our problem-solving journey, we can distance ourselves from the emotion and chaos surrounding the actual problem, deliberately managing our attention through creative techniques to locate, define and solve the problem.

The PSP wheel offers us the same advantages as a helicopter does to the commander overflying the battlefield. We can choose to get physically involved in the firefights on the ground, raising morale by our presence; but by viewing the battle from the air, we have the opportunity to see the big picture, and manage our resources of time, people and attention, to win the battle with the least cost.

The PSP wheel makes it possible for us to manage our tactics with the background of a sound strategic model. With a sound methodology, we can keep our attention on the particular tactics of our problem-solving area, while keeping an eye on the overall strategy, ensuring that we balance our attention across the whole process of the wheel.

The eight areas of the PSP wheel are as follows:

1   Identify Problem
2   Gather Data

7

3	Analyse Data
4	Generate Solutions
5	Select Solutions
6	Plan
7	Test and Rehearse
8	Action

One of the central themes behind the structure and content of the PSP wheel has been to combine simplicity with accessibility. A search of any reasonable management or education library will provide many problem-solving structures, but experience has taught me that problem-solving is usually a stressful business, and if you cannot remember a process sufficiently well to picture it in your head, interpret it and locate yourself within it, you just will not use it.

A quick look at the eight areas shows an interest beyond that of the traditional creativity theoreticians: an emphasis upon the problems of planning and implementation as well as developing ideas to solve the problem. This comes out of an interest in why good ideas can still fail, an issue which is discussed later.

The minimal objective of this handbook will have been met if, before an assignment or a meeting, you draw the wheel and use some of the eight areas to manage your own creative process, overcoming the traditionally impoverished problem-solving styles of most managers.

The eight stages in the wheel fall into three sub-processes: foundation, generation and execution.

FIGURE 2.1 THE THREE CREATIVE SUB-PROCESSES WITHIN THE PSP WHEEL

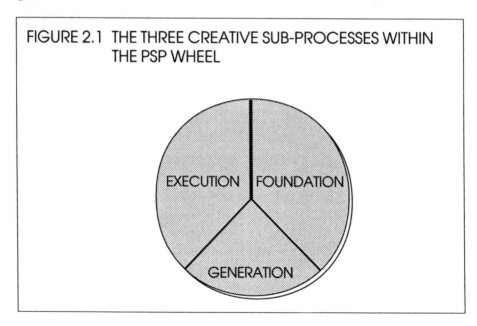

FOUNDATION

1   Identify Problem
2   Gather Data
3   Analyse Data

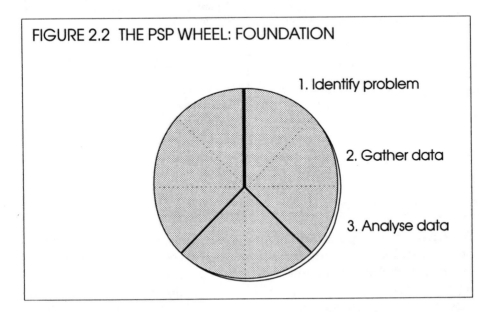

FIGURE 2.2 THE PSP WHEEL: FOUNDATION

1. Identify problem

2. Gather data

3. Analyse data

You draft an initial problem-statement, gather and analyse some data to confirm it, and discover that your initial definition is inaccurate; you repeat the process and again, the problem appears to mutate. Up to 80 per cent of your time can be spent just exploring this iterative sub-process.

Sometimes I am asked why I bother to distinguish between gathering and analysing data. The answer is that we tend to gather data that supports the implicit idea we have already (consciously or subconsciously) chosen. It is important to gather data openly without the ulterior motive of justifying an already-fixed idea of the problem and its solution. That is why I distinguish between the activities of gathering and analysing data: get hold of the data first; then and only then, ask yourself what does it tell you?

GENERATION

4   Generate Solutions
5   Select Solution

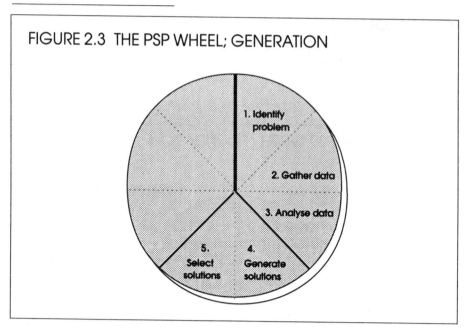

FIGURE 2.3 THE PSP WHEEL; GENERATION

We have another potential creative cycle founded on a well-defined problem-statement coming out of areas 1–3. We understand the problem and can have fun developing and capturing many ideas, each of which has to be discussed and developed before testing to select the best. We may find that our choice has weaknesses and accordingly, we may have to return to the foundation areas to gather more data or reinterpret the problem.

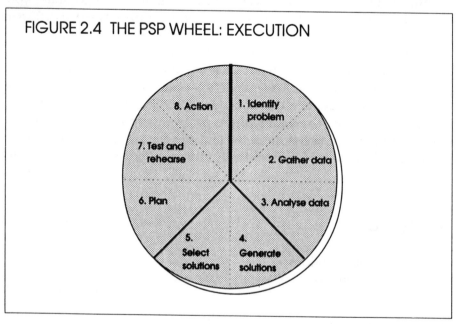

FIGURE 2.4 THE PSP WHEEL: EXECUTION

EXECUTION

6   Plan
7   Test and rehearse
8   Action

Taking our best idea, we develop a plan, using our creativity to anticipate all the obstacles and minor problems that may emerge. We consider our plan in terms of risk and, by testing the plan in all its detail, develop an awareness of detail and contingencies. This concentrates the mind, and in a team, fosters true teamwork and trust. The rehearsal in whatever form, helps us to visualize the activities and tune our behaviours to deliver success. I've included the final stage, Action, because all too often we race toward completion and its physical activity as a way of driving away anxiety, by losing ourselves in doing as opposed to thinking. There is a strong tendency to move straight into action, it draws and tempts us and the PSP reflects it as a danger when approached prematurely.

Remember that the wheel is not a linear process. Sometimes we may have to move backwards, in order to make the next step forward. When working around the wheel, the idea is to work forwards as well as backwards, iteratively. When making a transition, it is a good idea to check that everyone agrees to the move: either backwards, forwards or skipping to another position on the PSP wheel. The key is to know where you are, and develop your own discipline to manage your own thinking process.

Finally, let's put all three sub-processes together into the eight-area PSP wheel:

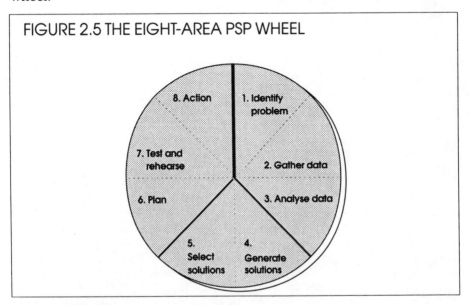

FIGURE 2.5 THE EIGHT-AREA PSP WHEEL

3

PROBLEM-SOLVING STYLES

❖

While the way we appear to solve problems according to the profile may be influenced by recent experience or even lack of it, I have noted three general stereotypes or tendencies in managers' problem-solving styles. I call them the Coyote, the Competitor and the Eagle.

STYLE 1: THE COYOTE

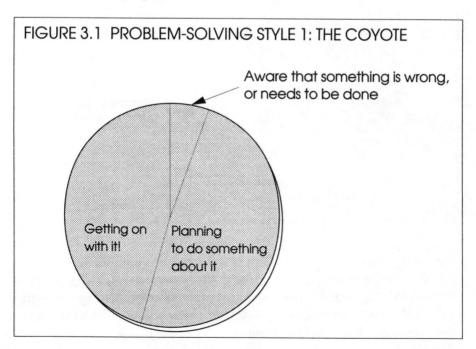

FIGURE 3.1 PROBLEM-SOLVING STYLE 1: THE COYOTE

Aware that something is wrong, or needs to be done

Getting on with it!

Planning to do something about it

The Coyote tends to go straight into planning (PSSP, stage 6). Once some general awareness of a problem situation exists, the Coyote develops a plan which translates into getting right in there and into implementation. The Coyote is characterized by a tendency to operate from a very restricted repertoire. Coyotes become stressed very quickly, and find it difficult to endure the ambiguity and uncertainty involved in defining the 'real' problem at the heart of the situation. They reduce the resulting stress of confronting and thinking about the situation by tending to see the problem they want to see. Data-gathering is a retrospective activity, justifying the idea they already had. They operate on 'gut-feel', and tend to say things like 'let's go for it!' They are inclined to overlook risk and find it difficult to anticipate or visualize danger or weaknesses in the plan and its details. As a result they tend to fasten onto the very first idea that appears.

STYLE 2 : THE COMPETITOR

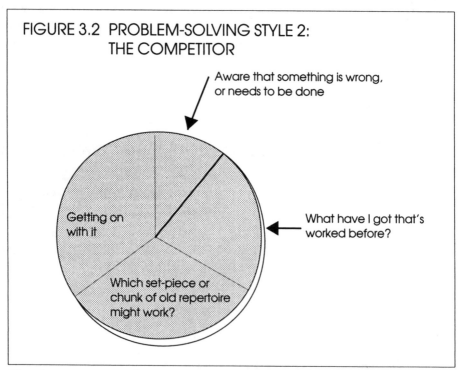

FIGURE 3.2 PROBLEM-SOLVING STYLE 2:
         THE COMPETITOR

Aware that something is wrong, or needs to be done

Getting on with it

What have I got that's worked before?

Which set-piece or chunk of old repertoire might work?

The Competitor tends to move past defining the problem and launches into having ideas (stage 4), but these ideas involve imposing solutions from an existing repertoire, irrespective of the problem. The question they are really asking themselves is not 'how many solutions can I think of?', but 'what can I throw at the problem?'

Their tendency to deploy a fixed repertoire no matter what the problem, means that running a traditional brainstorming session with them can tell you more about them as people and their obsessions than help to generate creative ideas. Competitors may be extensively trained professionals, who may have the tendency to see the world from the perspective of that profession, and only from that perspective. They will only consider breaking out of their repertoire-collection when they have exhausted its contents. Some studies of successful entrepreneurs confirm the competitor as a significant feature. Competitors' faith in the centrality of their existing repertoire of solutions reduces their feelings of vulnerability and stress.

They may have only one significant idea and spend their life developing and selling it. Circumstances may combine to make their idea live, but as time passes they continue to market this one idea well past its prime and may end up as either case-studies, guests on late-night talkshows or hermits!

They tend to see problem-solving as a very personal test of their own 'right stuff': as a challenge to their personal ideology. They are solution, not problem-centred.

STYLE 3: THE EAGLE

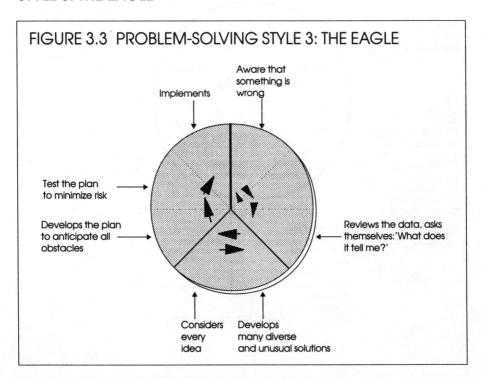

FIGURE 3.3 PROBLEM-SOLVING STYLE 3: THE EAGLE

Implements

Aware that something is wrong

Test the plan to minimize risk

Develops the plan to anticipate all obstacles

Reviews the data, asks themselves:'What does it tell me?'

Considers every idea

Develops many diverse and unusual solutions

The Eagle deliberately runs an iterative micro-cycle around stages 1–3, (from Identify problem, through Gather data to Analyse data), reformulating several statements of what the problem is, each time becoming more precise. The Eagle only moves into Generate solutions (stage 4) when satisfied with the definition of the problem and the data that supports it. The Eagle always develops at least three solutions for consideration, and distinguishes solutions into two types: first, process or 'how' the solution will be conducted, and second, novel ideas about 'what' could be done.

It is arguable that a problem-solving style should match the situation. The point of developing and discussing these stereotypes is that some individuals cannot choose their style. Most are either Coyotes or Competitors or somewhere in-between. The intention of this book is to

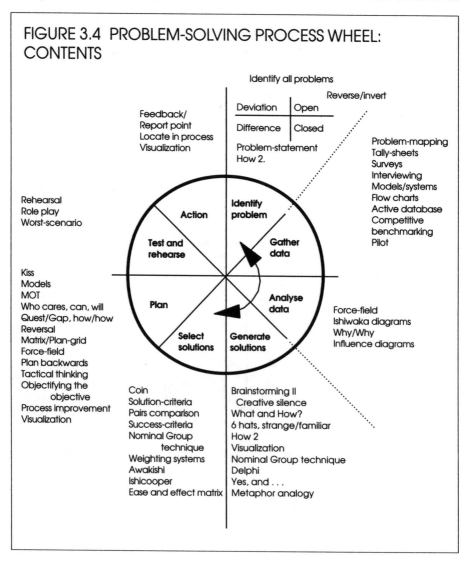

FIGURE 3.4 PROBLEM-SOLVING PROCESS WHEEL: CONTENTS

help managers to be clear about where they are now, and consider developing themselves into being more balanced problem-solvers, capable of fitting their problem-solving style to the context.

In Figure 3.4 the wheel contents are broken down into the eight areas, reflecting the structure of this book.

PART II

AN INTRODUCTION TO PROBLEM-SOLVING

❖

4

THINKING ABOUT PROBLEM-SOLVING

JUST WHAT IS A PROBLEM?

There are at least four ways of defining a problem: to distinguish a problem as being either a deviation, a matter of difference, open or closed.

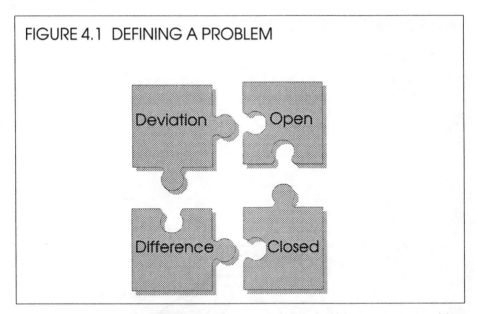

FIGURE 4.1 DEFINING A PROBLEM

A performance **deviation** is where something odd or unexpected has occurred. A matter of **difference** is the gap between where we are, and where we want to go.

Deviation and difference are not mutually exclusive. Deviation is the basis for defining problems in quality manufacturing or service industry environments involving control of a work or manufacturing process through the application of statistical process control. The first problem-analysis stage in Kepner-Tregoe's influential 'new rational manager' is called the 'deviation statement', linking a specific object with a malfunction which we wish to explain.

Difference is the basic problem-solving or 'gap' model: looking at where we are, and where we would like to be, and then analysing that gap in terms of the obstacles which we have to overcome within it.

An **open** problem is one without a 'correct' solution, and a **closed** problem is one which can be precisely defined, and has clear parameters and a 'correct' solution. The idea of solution 'correctness' pre-empts all our initiatives to introduce creativity into a problem-solving situation. In reality, no problem is truly 'open': it is our task to map the relative openness of how those affected by the problem perceive the problem and to map their often unstated perceptions of what constitutes a 'solution'.

In other words, we build up a picture of the world surrounding the solution by encouraging people to answer the questions: 'what would tell you that the problem had been solved?' or 'how would you know the problem had been solved?'

LEVELS OF PROBLEM-SOLVING

Problem-solving is not just a question of deviation, difference, openness or relative closedness, but also a question of the **level** within the organization at which problem-solving happens to be recognized, who sees it

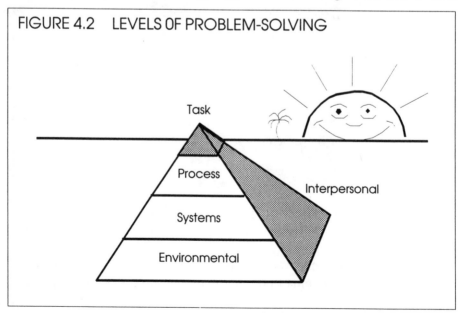

FIGURE 4.2   LEVELS OF PROBLEM-SOLVING

and how it is expressed. Sometimes the culture of the organization does not provide the language to express the problem. The greatest enemy of problem-solving is the way we can distance ourselves from seeing the real problem, the way our mindsets (frozen perceptions, stereotypes or personal myths) can mean we institutionalize problems by continuing to deal with symptoms and by ignoring fundamental causes which come from systems operating in the environment.

It can be useful to consider problems in terms of problem-solving levels.

Problem-solving levels are like the problem of what to do with an organizational 'dead cat' (that is, a problem which no one wants to touch because it may mean confronting powerful people or values within the culture).

Often a problem is initially seen as a mere task. A team is formed to manage the task of dealing with a problem. The team works together and realizes that the task is dealing with a symptom of a deeper problem. The team begins to redefine the problem. The problem begins to have a life of its own, and in the form of a symptom escapes out of its original functional frame, reframing through the 'process' level to that of 'system': where the problem is not to bury the dead cats you and your colleagues stumble upon, or to improve on the burial process or necessary team-working involved, but to find out where the dead cats come from, and just *who* is getting paid to make and introduce waste in the form of dead cats into the system of the organization?

MINDSETS, THINKING AND PROBLEM-SOLVING

'Mindset' is a term for the robot element in our thinking behaviour. A robot is useful when it recognizes the cues for some types of behaviour, like danger, but is dangerous when it ignores other cues or when the environment changes, like applying the routine of the Green Cross code in a country where they drive on the right.

You can generally tell when you have encountered a mindset within a discussion when a topic is raised which leads to emotional, attacking and dismissing behaviours. Most typically, the more you ask the question 'Why?', the more exasperated the person becomes because they either cannot answer or feel embarrassed about articulating an answer that places them outside a socially-accepted view of the world. At this point, you realize that you have run into a structure through which the individual views the world, a reference-point or landmark which helps that individual make sense of their world and out of which they have developed a practical theory of reality, linking observable effects with causes within their environment. The emotion encountered when we begin to question the basis of the mindset is entirely understandable. We are all capable of this kind of behaviour, it just depends upon the topic. After all, if you attempt to study and deconstruct my mindset, you are interfering with my reality: where I stand in it, who I think I am, and where I believe I come from.

It is possible to view problem-solving as an examination of how we process and arrange data into meaningful patterns or information. Imagine the mind as a kind of processing-surface, in the form of a tray of cool, jelly-like material, and the data introduced onto that surface as a hot, dark liquid. When we pour some hot data onto the surface we create a shape or pattern where the two have combined, which we can then scoop out, creating an impression.

A subsequent pouring of hot, dark data will add to the shape, but generally we find that it is our initial shape that determines how subsequent data is processed or shaped into information via the surface.

If we continue the metaphor of this data-shaping mechanism, it is our old way of shaping things which determines the type of inputs we can accept, the way we interpret them and determines or reflects the repertoire of available responses. Similarly, the more you visit competitors' organizations the more you realize that you were not even aware that you had a problem, until you saw other people's solutions.

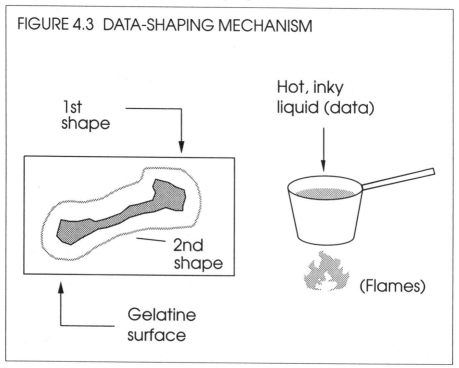

FIGURE 4.3 DATA-SHAPING MECHANISM

1st shape

2nd shape

Gelatine surface

Hot, inky liquid (data)

(Flames)

Daniel Isenberg (1984, 1986) studied the cognitive process used by managers when understanding or solving business problems. He found that managers tend to make decisions on incomplete data, even when additional useful data is available, using their experience to interpret problems, ignoring relevant data when presented. Managers operate out of a limited problem-solving perspective, only solving the next problem as it appears, instead of thinking all the way through to the objective by visualizing a complete flow of enabling problems which take them there.

If you reflect upon your own experience or study history, you find examples of this. The secret history of failed projects is often based upon a combination of all these elements of behaviour, whether by individuals, teams or committees. But why is this?

Problem-solving is a stressful activity. Since we prefer to avoid stress, we tend to reduce what I call the 'stress-gap': the period of time that exists between the arrival of a problem and its resolution through some planned activity. The exception to this is the crisis-driven manager who has become addicted to the adrenalin rush which extended stress brings, actively seeking and manufacturing the opportunity to indulge in it. To this end, we reduce our experience of this stress-gap through:

○   **Stereotyping**: seeing what we want or expect to see
○   **Repertoire**: only operating out of an established repertoire of preferred solutions
○   **Visibility**: we are unable to even see our problem exists until we discover someone else who has seen it, and managed to solve it
○   **Restricted perspective**: avoiding the stressful business of visualizing the sheer size and scale of the problem, by reducing our perspective down to only seeing the next, emergent activity as a problem.

This means that we tend to apply solutions on the basis of only approximate recognition of problems. We classify problems and apply our repertoire according to the general, recognizable shape that it seems to present. We do this because to investigate the problem and to understand it, is simply the most stressful thing we can do since it serves to delay action.

If we return to the information-shaping mechanism metaphor introduced earlier, an interesting aspect of it is the way that our repertoire and our central shaping mechanism tend to reflect each other, until they begin to seem like two facets of the same object which we might call an operational theory of action.

When we extend this idea to the area of developing an individual's problem-solving or thinking ability, it is his or her operational theory of action which we have to take into account.

My experience of leading training evaluation programmes in a large corporation brought me close to the problem of measuring the impact of our training upon individual managers and business performance. Initially, it was very hard to gain any objective evidence of the practice of new techniques or thinking processes within the business environment; but once I introduced evaluation as a component of the training process instead of an add-on, we began to measure a tremendous 'hardening' of the data: managing to connect the training content unambiguously with specific behaviours and measurable impacts within the business. The key lesson is that we cannot change the central shaping-mechanism, but we can introduce a useful level of stress into the situation, raising the level of individual attention of individuals to new opportunities for applying a more developed repertoire or thinking-process, for at least a time. In this way, the evaluation became part of the process of concentrating the individual's attention and adding value to the business by extending the initial repertoire through the training and reinforcing it.

The failure to understand stress and use it positively within project management is the reason why project managers tend to avoid thinking themselves into developing the full stream of purposeful activities which relate to each other and which together, deliver the project. It is simply too stressful to spend time gathering data to understand and visualize the whole problem, far less to spend time analysing it. It is much easier to blame the project management methodology than to confront your own failure to think in detail. The implicit decision to allow yourself to fail is much more comfortable to live with than deciding to succeed. If you decide to succeed, you have to carry a load of responsibility for designing your own behaviour to deliver the success you want.

It can be very useful to gain some idea of the stress-gaps organizational culture may impose upon individuals and teams.

In some organizations the priority is to do everything at the double, irrespective of the nature of the task. If you are working in a consultancy role and your client has a short stress-gap, in other words, they are unable to manage an extended period between the recognition of the problem and its resolution. You know that the final product will take some time, thus it may be useful to provide and publicly display a working prototype-solution incorporating all the functions and significant criteria required, as quickly as possible. Failure to do this can mean that by the time the solution actually arrives, the client no longer recognizes what they originally asked for: the absence of a prototype to focus attention having been filled by a collective organizational fantasy about the purpose of the project which may have evolved over a period of time. If you leave a vacuum, people tend to fill it themselves with their own ideas.

The classic techniques of creative problem-solving need special conditions to escape from the mindset-structure: essentially, the stress-gap needs to be managed by relaxation and developing confidence in the problem-solving tools through practice, but also through the use of humour, manipulation of the problem, suspension of judgement and by deliberately changing our perspective of how we view and express the problem.

PROBLEM-SOLVING AND LEARNING

By solving problems we can learn. We can demonstrate that we have learnt by the changes in behaviour we are prepared to adopt. To learn is to solve problems at many levels. To learn is to accept a constant process of sensitization and desensitization:

Sensitization   To new cues for behaviours, and

Desensitization   To the fear and discomfort of consciously breaking out of mindsets, old and inflexible thinking-structures or theories, repertoires or old ways of working.

It is possible to see this taken to extremes:

> I once had to deal with both extremes within the context of a challenging out-door management development course being run for a client's top-management team: one participant had become very depressed in the immediate aftermath of attending a course, and begun to damage himself, much to the horror of their immediate family. This was an extreme form of sensitization brought on by the power of the 'temporary institution' or small-group/hot-house confrontational, group-process courses that strive to help individuals to gain insight into their own behaviours and impact on others. This manager remained traumatized and sensitive for a long time. I investigated and discovered that the tutors running the course had become desensitized to the behaviour and feelings of the partici-pants, to the extent that they had developed their own informal measurement-system: whereby a 'powerful' course was measured among their fellow-tutors as one where someone broke down and cried in public.
>
> Going deeper, this manager had been so stressed throughout the course that he had not slept at all. Interviewing other past participants, I began to discover a darker history of post-course resignation from the organization and ongoing trauma which was not being addressed, going back over several years.
>
> A typical incident was an exercise scheduled for the second night of this 5-day course: the long, night abseil. Typically, this involved everyone being offered a series of activities to gain 'points' for attractive items to facilitate survival over the remaining days of the course. The highest-scoring activity was a night abseil of 150 metres. This experience remained in many memories years after. The approach was usually in a minivan at night. On disembarking, the teams would be brought to the abseil point and a large rock was dropped over the edge into the dark abyss. The long silence before the shocking, echoing crash below, dramatically emphasized the depth of the abseil. Very quickly, the tutor would select a participant to go first. This participant was used to demonstrate the abseil system and how it was ultimately controlled by another tutor from a belay-point.

The participant would then be helped to the edge with their back to the abyss, lean into it, place their feet flat on the vertical wall, controlling the rope through the descending device on their harness. Most of the managers had never done this before. If you were lucky, the first to go might succeed without a hitch, but if you were unlucky, you would have a series of 'refusals' who would have to be recovered, often at the loss of all their dignity. Ultimately, this meant that for the remainder of the course you saw yourself as one of the few or sometimes one of the many who had 'failed'. Some felt this way for years afterwards.

I asked the tutors why we did this exercise. 'It's about learning' , they told me. I guessed they would say that. I continued, 'what do you mean?' 'Well, it is about overcoming your fear of the learning situation, and coming to terms with the new situation instead of rejecting change in the organization.' 'So it's about learning to manage the challenge of personal and organizational change?' 'Yes'.

In a way, they were right and I knew it. But people were becoming traumatized, and losing self-esteem through the clumsiness of the tutors who had become desensitized to the impact of the learning situation they controlled. They weren't selecting managers to become Special Forces, this wasn't supposed to be a rite of passage, but people were being scared and scarred.

Ultimately, the training organization's culture had become desensitized and needed to become sensitized to the situations they were using. I reversed the situation and ran a special course just for them, recreating this crisis in parallel learning situations using novel technologies and contexts they weren't familiar with to re-sensitize them to participants' emotions on such a course.

To learn is:

○   to accept the need for objectives and to plan to achieve them bit by bit.

○   to decide to adopt a proactive stance in an often chaotic environment.

○   to make a conscious decision to take on the problem of knowing and doing.

Is knowledge an end in itself, like a work of art?, or is knowledge about purpose? Is learning the process of mapping our knowledge so that we are more able to concentrate our thinking tools?

Managing our thinking-process requires that we learn to answer these questions, aware of the limitations of our maps and the theories which connect its features, and utilizing good functional tools or thinking-processes which enable us to rebuild the map and create yet further tools.

As the world of work continues to change, the constant pressure to learn is inescapable. Workers (and I include managers as workers) in quality industries are expected not to function merely as disposable cogs within a larger machine, but manage the outputs as well as the inputs, and monitor and improve the process of work itself. The conceptual level of work is rising. No longer can we accept work as a necessary evil between weekends. Like professional artists, we need to view our work as an extension of ourselves. This is my work – this is me.

CONVERGENT AND DIVERGENT THINKING

Solving problems requires the ability to recognize when to be logical and focus upon the process (convergent or closing-down) and when to defocus, to relax and deliberately escape from what may be a linear logic of viewing a problem head-on and to look at it from a new position (divergent or opening up the problem-situation).

> I was leading a project 400 miles from home, over a period of several months. Since most of the consultancy team lived in the same area, we shared a large car and drove to the site and back together. Travelling together had serious advantages. Going there, we could rehearse and develop our plan for the week, while driving home in a mood anticipating the weekend, we reviewed the project but also began to make jokes about it. These jokes were a way of viewing the project in a divergent way. The jokes often contained what turned out to be our best ideas and ultimately stimulated our most useful work.

WORKING WITH TEAMS

There are three basic situations when it is necessary for individuals to work together in groups:

Expertise When the problem requires a combination of several different types of expertise

Politics When you want to maximize the chance of having a solution accepted: a group can be more effective than an individual in convincing the directors of a company to adopt an innovative solution

Ownership When the group owns the problem and its outputs, and will have to implement a specific plan of action

The problem of working together productively in teams, is usually underrated and requires attention to the necessary disciplines. A shared problem-solving process is a key to channelling the team's understanding and scheduling their creativity.

WORKING TOGETHER WITHIN AN OVERALL PROBLEM-SOLVING PROCESS

Synectics (see Gordon and Prince) is a problem-solving approach among many, which came to terms with the realization that creative problem-solving can be a very social activity. Synectics is a way of packaging creative problem-solving techniques which pays attention to the group/ meeting process by having explicit process leadership, clear roles, planned structure to sessions and the use of routines to create a support-ive environment.

All problem-solving sessions require an initial contextual, problem-focusing (the what, who, where and when), identification of problem-owners (the who) and an explicit process to manage the journey to the solution (the how).

You may have to plan your leadership of the problem-solving process rather like a 'Kentucky Preacher', that is: 'tell 'em what you're going to tell 'em, tell 'em, then tell 'em what you told 'em.' In other words, make the problem-solving process explicit.

To do this, draw the process onto a flipchart. Besides appearing to be spontaneous, if we work with an explicit process we have the ability to locate ourselves within it, gaining confidence as we progress. We can use a piece of Blu-tack to locate ourselves within it (going forward and back-ward, leap-frogging stages when necessary). The Blu-tack marker is use-ful for refocusing the team when it inadvertently moves into normal meeting mode: expressing cynicism or helplessness, saying 'ain't it a shame', expressing powerlessness or inability to take action or escaping from the purpose by bringing up irrelevances which belong outside the purpose of the team.

It is important to remember that people's attentions tune out as well as into the group meeting. Individuals may nod and smile, but they may be actually tuning out of the meeting, and thinking about windsurfing at Vassiliki or climbing in the Pyrenees. When they tune in again, the posi-tion of the Blu-tack on the problem-solving process will show them where the team is now, and enable them to participate again without embarrass-ing themselves.

The Blu-tack blob locates us within the problem-solving process and helps us to plan our approximate movement through the stages of the process, helping to reduce the natural sense of panic which the stress-gap induces, stretching it out and diverting our energy out of panic and old negative comfort routines into controlled creativity. Using a pre-pared, professionally-produced, printed and laminated PSP chart reduces people's willingness to feel that they can reinterpret it into their own language, ask questions, use it flexibly and improve it. The other problem is that if you are going to use the PSP like a map and a piece of Blu-tack as an indicator of where you are within it, then individual PSPs used as a general reference by the team defeat the object of being able to focus everyone's attention onto one central model, with one piece of Blu-tack moving around it.

5

A QUESTION OF CREATIVITY

The ultimate purpose of creativity is to change ideas or create new ones. These two processes are often mixed up together but they can be separated as follows:

O   Escape from old ideas
O   Generation of new ideas.

Any study of deliberate, purposeful creativity is inevitably a study of thinking processes involved in problem-solving. One approach to creativity is to see it as a process involving information-gathering and processing, the recognition of existing patterns and the discovery of new patterns within existing data.

Creativity is escaping from old habits of thinking, responding to the stimulus of a problem in a novel way, formulating new combinations of ideas or fresh perspectives for viewing the problem.

It is important to recognize **when** and **where** to focus creative thinking. A classic collection of examples can be found in Ackoff's (1978) accounts of his consulting experiences, where creative solutions turned out to be unacceptable to his clients because they were unable to recognize them as solutions. They may have been capable of solving the problem but their very creativity made them unrecognizable and thus prevented them from being seen as practical solutions.

Creativity is escaping from being trapped – it is about movement.

OBSTACLES TO CREATIVITY

Any approach to creativity needs to confront and escape mindset-

31

structures by overcoming the interlocking and mutually supporting obstacles of

○　　The past
○　　Stress
○　　Coyote problem-solving
○　　Comfort.

The **past** determines much of our perception of what can be done – it conditions our recognition of 'correctness' in thinking which can disable creative thinking at the outset. By deliberate use of problem-solving processes we can choose to deal with our operational repertoire, our preferred way of doing things.

Experience means we tend to look for the key, recognizable cues which line up with our repertoire and allow us to switch it on. This can be the product of routine, of limited experience or imagination, or the inability to consider shifting to a new viewpoint from which to observe the problem.

As well as shaping much of our perception of what can be done, the past conditions our recognition of 'correctness' which can disable us by reducing our creative thinking mobility at the outset.

By deliberate use of problem-solving processes we can choose to manage our operational repertoire, aware of our preferred way of doing things, deliberately choosing when to break out of an established, set-piece repertoire.

As I have said earlier, when a problem appears, we experience some **stress**. We naturally dislike stress and try to keep the gap between the arrival of the problem and its resolution through action, as short as possible. How we manage ourselves within this stress-gap period can say a lot about us. Observation of individuals deliberately exposed to stressful, social problem-solving situations is the basis of many personnel-selection systems. The fear of taking risks, the tendency to reduce uncertainty by judging rather than generating ideas, the tendency to look for apparent consensus conforming to unstated group impressions of the problem and its solution all combine to influence our perception of correctness. This can be reversed and prove equally dangerous in the form of a distinct lack of fear.

Linked to the obstacle of the past, we also need to face up to the symptoms of stress by recognizing our tendency to displace our stress through irrelevant or 'tidying' behaviours. Sometimes children only keep their rooms tidy when examinations loom. This hygiene or tidying behaviour can also be evident in sorting activities or a tendency to deal with unimportant aspects of the problem first, instead of concentrating on the core of the problem. How many times have you found yourself dealing with the parts of a problem you wanted to deal with because you felt you recognized and could therefore handle them, while at the same time you were aware that you really should have been working on the part of the problem that you didn't understand?

I derived what I call the Coyote approach to solving problems from the popular Warner Brothers' Looney Tunes cartoons featuring the Coyote in pursuit of the Roadrunner. The Coyote pursues the Roadrunner through a series of comic crises based on his inability to have more than one idea at a time. The Coyote develops that one idea into a plan, which is in turn, implemented without any anticipation or rehearsal of weak points or dangers. The cartoons are funny because they are predictable. Unfortunately, many managers operate in the same way. They may work in a distracting environment which has itself been engineered by continual fire-fighting, producing cyclical crises which are never completely resolved, and where no one ever gets to solve the real problem. The Coyote is very busy. And that's just the way Coyotes like it.

The antithesis of stress is **comfort**. We can derive great comfort from the culture of the organization in which we work. Our working culture can mean that we can become trapped into inflexible, formal, thinking processes. Similarly, organizational roles can produce a public, symbolic decision-style: that is, at this level in the organization, you have to show your fitness to be considered a real manager by taking decisions of a particular type, aligned with the management culture of your organization.

We need to regulate our need for comfort and our tendency to cling to the first idea that occurs without developing alternatives, when facing the deliberate journey into the unknown required by creative problem-solving. One way of looking at the process of creativity is that of the creative journey analogy. Imagine yourself in a thick wood. You are lost, so you follow the first track you encounter. Eventually you find yourself at a meeting of several tracks. Which should you take?

The problem of the creative problem-solver is similar. You have several choices before you. Which should you take? The difficulty is that all the routes could be wrong for you. The answer is to move yourself to a position which allows you to make a real choice, a piece of ground which gives you a perspective from which you can see the whole landscape, and can use your process binoculars to select not only the best route, but also the best destination. In order to move to the new perspective or viewpoint, we will have to expose ourselves above the tree-line, abandon the well-trodden paths to find a vista which may itself be frightening: offering too many choices of destinations and routes.

When Robin Williams' English teacher encouraged his pupils to stand on their desks in the film *Dead Poets Society*, he best captured the idea of deliberately escaping from the frustrations of limited vision, and moving to a creative viewpoint. By using a clear process to manage our movement forward to the solution, without fitting the solution to the problem, we can creatively solve the real problem.

The following story illustrates the four obstacles, while emphasizing the need to be able to shift perspective:

> One of my sadder consultancy assignments was to review an engineering organization's strategy, and outline the way forward. The managing director was not sanguine about this assignment and I could tell that the board had imposed me on him much against his will. Nevertheless, I persevered partly out of reverence for the history of British manufacturing and the still-great name this company had. He (the MD) felt he had tried everything over the last 12 years: from delayering, cost then budget-centres, focused business-units, cut-backs, TQM, recruiting competitors' 'stars', through to joint-ventures on the Pacific Rim, and a supply-chain review with some competitive benchmarking that was probably going to lead to business process re-engineering.
>
> Ultimately, I made my presentation to the MD. He was a busy man but gave me two hours and was intrigued by my request for a TV and VCR. Characteristically, he took the initiative and asked what else was left for him to do? I began by pointing to a laminated A1-size wallchart of the organization structure and, putting a red overhead pen into his hand, asked him to circle those parts of the organization making a loss. He circled the engineering manufacturing units. I asked him to take a blue pen and indicate those units which made a profit. He put the blue pen down and waved at the rest of the structure. I asked him what the rest did? They sold engineering expertise in the form of consultancy to make products, but largely sold intellectual patents for products to manufacturers who made them themselves. I then asked him whether he had watched John Harvey-Jones' (JHJ) *Troubleshooter* series on BBC. He particularly remembered the Morgan cars episode. I asked him why the Morgan family had stonewalled JHJ throughout the episode. I put to him that the real problem was that JHJ had not understood what Morgan was selling – what the real product was. His imposing his manufacturing mindset onto making the cars faster to make more money was based on a misunderstanding of the product which was not the Morgan car, but the *idea* of the car. This idea was so powerful that it eclipsed the need to have the car when you wanted it. People were prepared to wait, and in fact the waiting had become an indistinguishable component within the structure of the product itself, a component which could only be devalued through a traditional marketing approach within a niche-market.
>
> I suggested we left the room, and walked around the manufacturing-site. 'OK, but how does this apply to me and my business?' he asked. I reminded him about the wallchart. 'Whatever you really do, it's not manufacturing in the strict, old sense as you knew it. You might as well save the money and close those sites down. You know the real work is being done on the CAD/CAM system defining products which you sell to other people who want to make them. The future is in developing expertise and selling ideas to partners in new markets. The basis of your strength was always intellectual, it just got confused with actually making things yourself, which you cannot do and still make a profit.' We stared at the large empty sheds together.
>
> I was lucky, I didn't own the problem, I could stand outside and see it. Two weeks later, I read in the *Financial Times* that he had been replaced.

Human perception is strongly influenced by what the perceiver expects to see, and these expectations can interfere with the process of creative problem-solving. One approach to facilitating creative thinking is to be aware of these obstacles to creativity and then consciously use techniques to overcome them.

HOW DO YOU KNOW WHEN YOU ARE WORKING CREATIVELY?

You know that you are working creatively when you deliberately use a process to overcome the obstacles to creativity. Creativity is based on two words: **strange** and **familiar**

The words 'strange' and 'familiar' are the basis of generating new ideas. When we begin to generate new ideas by using these words, we can transform the way we look at or interpret familiar problems either by deliberately abstracting the problem from its familiar context to make it 'strange', or by using a 'familiar' process change our own position to view the problem from a new perspective.

An example of shifting perspective on a problem is the nine-dot problem (Figure 5.1):

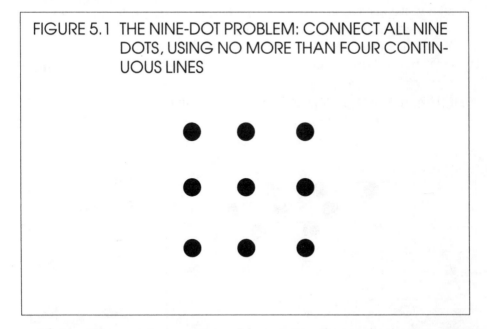

FIGURE 5.1 THE NINE-DOT PROBLEM: CONNECT ALL NINE DOTS, USING NO MORE THAN FOUR CONTINUOUS LINES

After much experimentation and arguments about what constitutes a line, and how you define continuous lines (one after another), people generally come up with the idea of beginning to draw the four continuous lines from outside the 'box' formed by the nine-dot formation (Figure 5.2).

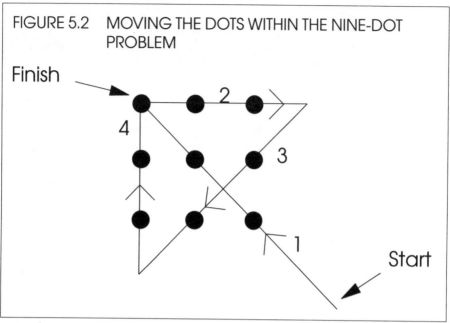

FIGURE 5.2   MOVING THE DOTS WITHIN THE NINE-DOT
                       PROBLEM

At this point, everyone sighs with understanding and relief. But the point needs to be made that perhaps this demonstrates only a first level of creativity. *We need to stand outside the borders of the problem, in order to see it properly and connect it up as a whole.*

Often when this exercise has been used to make this point, people start to use it as a sort of intellectual shorthand, to distinguish between 'in-the-

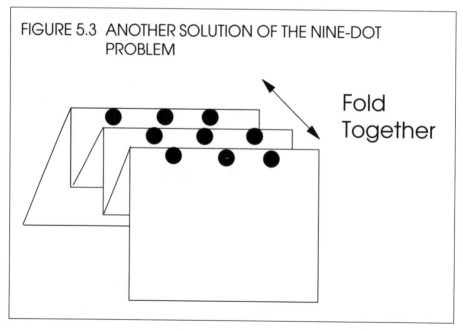

FIGURE 5.3 ANOTHER SOLUTION OF THE NINE-DOT
                      PROBLEM

box' thinking of someone who has preserved the perspective of someone who sits within the problem, and 'out-of-the-box' thinking: where people have deliberately chosen to look at the problem from outside, to see it in a new light.

We can of course, go further and stretch ourselves intellectually by reducing the number of continuous lines from four to only three lines.

We can connect all nine dots by pleating the paper (as in Figure 5.3) and virtually superimposing the dots over each other, then drawing only three continuous lines (Figure 5.4).

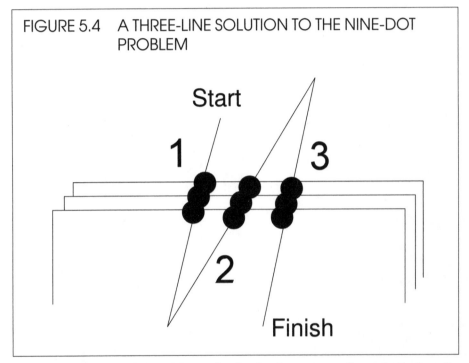

FIGURE 5.4   A THREE-LINE SOLUTION TO THE NINE-DOT PROBLEM

Although you will be able to think of other ways of manipulating the medium onto which the dots are drawn to connect the nine dots, we can usefully use this example to demonstrate a second level of creativity, that is, *by changing the nature of the relationship between the components of the problem, we can connect them in a novel way.*

Similarly, by using an analytical routine or problem-solving process to construct, deconstruct and redefine the problem, we can introduce a familiar logic to make the problem 'strange' and more open to analysis and manipulation.

The eight stages of the problem-solving process are described area-by-area in Part III.

PART III

THE PROBLEM-SOLVING PROCESS

❖

Stage 1

IDENTIFY THE PROBLEM

'Almost any problem can be solved that can be adequately expressed'
The Glossary, IBM

With complex problems, you can find yourself spending up to 80 per cent of your time iteratively working out of temporary problem-statements which are updated and reviewed through waves of data-gathering and analysis. The problem can begin to seem like some hostile, alien life-form which appears to mutate in response to every weapon you use against it.

As we said in the Introduction to Problem-Solving, apart from a problem being relatively open or closed, the word 'problem' is ambiguous, since we can see it as a deviation (something's gone wrong and we want it fixed, or we want to understand why it's happened), and as a difference (how do we get there?, how do we make the shift to where we want to be?).

Deviation requires us to map the system that produces the symptom, and difference means we have to anticipate all the obstacles along the journey to success. In the PSP wheel, we require both types of thinking. We may start by puzzling over the difference/symptom, but we have to be able to complete the cycle with an implementation, which is a problem in itself.

1 SIMPLE PROBLEM-STATEMENTS

It is unlikely that the problem-statement can be agreed at the outset. Writing a problem-statement is rather like raising a battle-flag. It is a symbolic act showing the level of seriousness and commitment to action felt by the team.

It is important that a project team agrees a problem-statement which is short, clear, and unambiguous, and includes a definable measure of successful performance. For example, 'The problem is to increase sales of product X by 10 per cent within 12 months'.

Failure to state the problem and revisit the statement as the team progresses in its problem-solving process will lead to a lack of focus and motivation. The team *must* have a problem-statement before entering the stage of Generating Solutions.

2 HOW TO (H2)

'How To' statements help us to experiment with formulating the problem or problems into an accessible shape. They help us to answer the questions 'what is the problem we want to solve?' and 'how is it best expressed so that we understand it, and can begin to solve it?'

H2 requires a problem-solver to adopt an attitude of mind which asks two preliminary questions: What do I want? and What stops me getting what I want? These questions are followed by H2 statements which suggest how to overcome those obstacles and achieve those goals.

The way you express the H2 statements can use metaphor to capture the imagination. When you are working on a problem, the greater the variety in your list of different H2 statements and the more likely you are to identify the key problem by making an emotional connection that rings true, that is, a direct connection which shows a new way, or even several new routes into the problem. Three H2 case-studies give an insight into how useful the approach can be.

H2 STUDY 1

The Sales organization of an international corporation was facing declining sales and market-share. They believed that by working on the way the selling-process was managed internally, significant financial improvements could be realized. Service and maintenance units were dubious about Sales division leadership since it was a) their idea, b) they were probably responsible for the poor figures, declining market-share and customer-base, c) the reward system was seen as biased toward Sales, and d) Sales tended to blame the support and maintenance units for failure.

Goal:	To introduce an integrated, focused approach to selling products
Obstacles:	Functional specialisms, boundary-management and reward systems

H2	*Metaphor/Analogy*
	H2 be a customer
	H2 think like a customer
	H2 walk in their shoes
H2 focus on delivering the customers' needs	H2 be in the shoes of the customer
H2 switch our attention away from ourselves and political boundary-watching, and onto gaining and protecting market-share	H2 find the door into the customer
H2 create a relationship with the customer	H2 build the door
H2 know what he wants/is thinking	H2 open the door
	H2 have our own key
H2 get into the customer's decision-making process	
H2 become part of the way they run their business	H2 become adopted by them
H2 make it our business	H2 be part of their family
H2 demonstrate our value-add to their business-process	H2 become a relative
	H2 be the Cadbury's milk-tray man
H2 manage the entry of our internal units into the customer without fallouts.	H2 have a family resemblance
H2 walk and talk like them	

Discussion

This was an interesting problem. The whole experience validated the problem-solving levels model: we started working on the problem at the level of a task, which then became a problem of process and ultimately one of system.

The key obstacles to clarity were the nature of the organization, the source of the initiative and the strong 'me-too-ism' of its Sales culture. At no time did they ever discuss whether they were making products that the customer actually needed. As with other international computer manufacturers up until 1990, there was a strong agenda supporting the manufacture of a complete product-range of which only a minority delivered the profit, as opposed to the niche-focused products being produced by an upstart competitor. The H2 statements pursued a strong 'Sales' theme or bias, because Sales traditionally supplied company leadership and had taken on the initiative of reviewing the selling-process which was naturally within their remit.

Although they were willing to take strong medicine, they found the output of the sessions rather frightening because it led them to question the nature of their relationship with customers. If the organization wanted to get closer to the customer, to develop a relationship so that they could know what the customer needed and was thinking, they had to become an integral part of the way the customer ran their business. Such a key person would have to 'belong' that is, be the kind of person who could contribute to the business strategy meetings that drove the decisions to select the technology to deliver the business strategy. This new kind of salesperson would have to be able to demonstrate their fitness to be in that kind of meeting, perhaps even able to facilitate a strategy process without necessarily selling product at the end of it. In other words, the customer had to be able to see some significant value-add in having this new type of salesperson at the heart of their strategy process, influencing both the technology-definition phase and the implementation. Looking at the environment in which this new salesperson would operate, Sales realized that they had to concentrate on recruiting someone who talked boardroom language, looked like a director, mingled with them socially, perhaps had a similar career-profile instead of a career selling computers within one company.

We compromised toward the end. Sales realized that the old conditions of a naïve market to sell into had changed. Customers were wiser now, often having gone through as many as three technology waves in as little as five years. Ultimately, Sales decided to begin the transition, by reviewing the way the business met customer needs. I made the point that their mindset about their selling process involved waiting at the end of a long tube, down which came products they had to sell. Manufacturing timing to introduce products was not connected to customer timing in terms of when they wanted it. What we had to do was to influence the nature of what came down the tube, as well as who sold it at corporate level, and ultimately redesign the selling-process. This last idea came firmly out of the metaphors generated, and proved fruitful. We learned much about the selling-process, its data-corruption, its flawed reward system, the way it encouraged duplication, its complex routing for signing-off, and the way it was used to pay off internal political debts.

H2 STUDY 2

A business had just undergone a review by its bank in order to secure a £3M loan to fund its increased activity within Europe. The business had to pay £100K for this review. The report misrepresented some ideas as plans, and the data-gathering process was lengthy, painful and disruptive.

Goal:	To develop a painless relationship with the bank.
Obstacles:	We don't understand each other's needs.

H2:	*Metaphor/Analogy*
H2 prevent this ever happening again	H2 prevent extensive, intrusive investigative surgery
H2 ensure future consultants get to know the things we want them to know	
H2 know what the consultant needs	H2 monitor our own health
H2 run the business in a way that would make the consultant unnecessary	H2 be obviously healthy*
H2 find out what the bank wants and give it to them	
H2 brings the bank into the firm, so that we both get what we want	

Discussion

There was genuine emotion within this small company which centred on the consultancy experience. What had started out as a hobby in a lock-up garage by two postgraduates in electronic product design had grown into a serious business set to expand into Europe. They had taken their relationship with the bank for granted from their earliest days, and felt that the trust they assumed had been developed over time in their relationship had been thrown away by the bank through the imposition of the consultancy's investigation of their business. Similarly, they were angry at having to include the cost of the bank's consultants in their projected loan: having to borrow the money to pay the consultancy in order to borrow further to develop the business. Their anger initially came from a sense of betrayal, but also from what was seen as the consultants' misrepresentation of what they had been told and the intrusive way the data for the report was gathered and interpreted.

The H2 statements included powerful medical metaphors, involving pain, leading from intrusive surgery through to the idea of being able to display the state of business health (we had a long discussion linking scurvy and limejuice as a minor diversion). The final decision – to bring the bank into the company – was developed by drawing out the relationship of bank: consultancy: company and then deleting the consultancy in order to have clear relationships between bank: company. Thus, both sides could get what they wanted without intermediaries. The decision was taken to have a much closer relationship with the bank's account manager, bringing him into company meetings on a formal basis, and understanding what the bank needed.

A footnote: The company had a mindset about its money-supply. They seemed to believe that only one bank could supply investment. The root of this blindness lay in the way not only the company, but also the bank had changed. As the company had grown, it had moved into a new category of borrowing-risk. The amount of perceived risk had changed the relationship, making it more impersonal, and the bank had become an extension of a centralized system that did not measure goodwill and trust.

H2 STUDY 3

The managing director of a factory was concerned that his manufacturing process was sometimes unpredictable, leading to waste and a need to employ supervisors in policing the output and re-working it before it could be delivered to customers.

Goal: To develop a predictable, manufacturing process.

Obstacles: Lack of knowledge about determinants of variability.

H2	*Metaphor/Analogy*
H2 control the manufacturing process so that the product quality is predictable	H2 bake a cake
H2 identify the key variables in the components' assembly process which make it predictable	H2 keep fish fresh (see discussion)
	H2 introduce a predator into the situation
	H2 become a predator
H2 move the problem	H2 become the customer
H2 motivate supplier to own and solve the problem of the process	

Discussion

This is a third example of a company experiencing change, and the second example of one where the business is attempting to compete within a changing market. This traditional manufacturing engineering organization had to deal not only with the unpredictable quality of its product, but with a customer who had changed their perception of quality and expected its traditional supplier to deliver products that worked, which didn't require modifications or rework and certainly wasn't prepared to pay for them on the basis of cost-plus or loss of valuable time.

In this case, the loss of a major customer would mean closure and redundancies. Although the problem of product-quality was understood intellectually, the engineering function approached the problem as though nothing could be done beyond expanding the quality inspection function. Something had to be done immediately, and a long-term solution would have to follow on.

We developed the metaphorical idea of birthday-cake baking as a parallel situation where failure would be socially embarrassing and unambiguous. We discussed the potential for failure and developed a model of successful, consistent birthday-cake baking. Unfortunately, the strategies that came out of this metaphor led to time-consuming attention to detail which would help in the long term, but wouldn't help us to blitz the problem in the short term.

At this point, I distracted everyone by telling the story of a company which caught, delivered, marketed and sold fresh fish. This fishmonger believed that selling the freshest fish would create competitive advantage for itself. They experimented, keeping the trapped fish alive and alert in the hold before landing, but ultimately they were told that the best way to maintain the freshness of the fish was to introduce a predator fish into the hold, keeping the fish stimulated until landing.

The managing director liked the idea of being the predator in his own factory, and thus fixing his workforce's attention on the manufacturing process (he had also seen Arnold Schwarzenegger in the film: *Predator*, and fancied himself as a man of action). Ultimately, we combined this predator role with the idea of moving the problem: instead of seeing himself as the supplier to the ultimate customer who used his products, he shifted perspective to become the customer of his own suppliers.

We developed this idea, which led to calling the suppliers of sub-assemblies and components into the problem and setting them a time-limit to solve the problem or face a loss of business themselves. This approach was wildly successful; it meant that for the first time the suppliers discovered what actually happened to their work when it was delivered to the factory for final assembly. Many weaknesses were remedied, the process became predictable and the quality-inspection function were redirected back into supporting the continuous improvement within the plant.

3 DEVIATION STATEMENT

In Kepner and Tregoe's analytical approach to problem-solving, a problem is a performance deviation: the difference between **should** and **actual**.

Should – Actual = Deviation

A deviation statement specifies an object, or class of objects with an associated shortfall in performance, or class of malfunction so that we can discover the reason for the relationship.

A deviation statement is supported by an analytical frame combining

is/is not and selective use of Kipling's 'six honest serving-men': 'What and Why and When and How and Where and Who.'

FIGURE S1.1 'WHAT AND WHY AND WHEN AND HOW AND WHERE AND WHO'

	IS	IS NOT
WHAT	is it?	isn't it?
WHERE	is it?	isn't it?
WHEN	does it happen?	doesn't it happen?
WHO	is involved?	isn't involved?
WHY	does it happen?	doesn't it happen all the time?
HOW (EXTENT)	big is it?	big could it be? Why isn't it bigger?

I have found similar analytical frames very useful for checking on and capturing expectations on long projects, ensuring that we are agreed upon the specification of the solution by agreeing not only on what the project *is*, but also what it definitely *isn't*.

4 IDENTIFY ALL PROBLEMS

In a complex, open problem you will find that the first three stages of the Problem-Solving Process tend to form an iterative sub-process in their own right:

This iterative loop will run through itself several times. To keep people on-track within the problem-solving process, use the Blu-tack, moving round until you finally arrive at a definitive problem statement.

FIGURE S1.2 THE PSP WHEEL: THE ITERATIVE LOOP

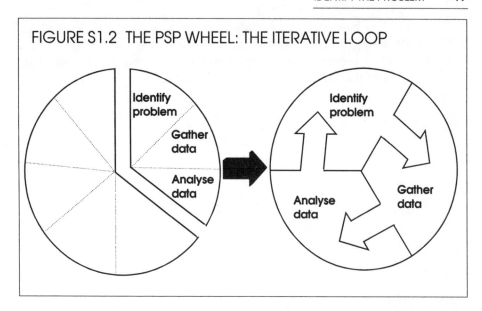

Before you go forward, it can be very useful to identify all the problems you face, and if possible, to prioritize them, adding these to the problem statement. Listing the problems will help you to **visualize** the obstacles to overcome, and **specify** the solution criteria. This exercise will also prepare the team for the necessary planning stage which must resolve all these problems, in the correct order.

FIGURE S1.3 DEVELOPING AN INFORMATION STRATEGY
PLAN (ISP)

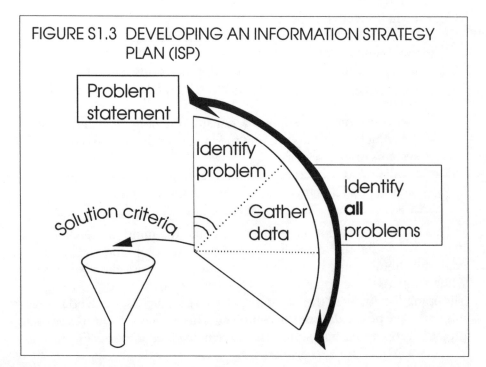

What follows is an example taken from a project to develop an Information Strategy Plan (ISP) for a leading company, which shows how we can develop our thinking about what a solution will look like and develop criteria for guiding our behaviour so as to support the way we manage such a project.

I WILL KNOW THAT THE ISP PROJECT HAS BEEN SUCCESSFUL BECAUSE:

○ I will know what information is needed to satisfy most of our needs.

○ I will be able to see a road that leads to the full involvement of our frontline supervisors in the ownership and delivery of the business plan.

○ I will actually see a real 'tool' for the management of this division that helps me to distinguish and concentrate on the really important issues.

○ It will give me a quick 'hit' in terms of delivering the key goals and objectives and help me to see common threads that run through the initiatives to deliver the goals.

○ I will have a workplan for my IS division which will be agreed by all functions and will not be identified as being purely Finance-driven.

○ I will know that I spent my money wisely.

○ It won't just be a consideration of the ISP but will identify the needs and how to satisfy them.

○ It will consider all the customers (internal and external), and the resulting prioritization system will integrate and reflect their needs.

○ I will get a menu of solutions, considering both ideal and practical, which takes into account the impact of the planned national systems on our system.

○ It will include guidance for implementing solutions (sequencing, timing, impact, dangers and how to overcome them).

This list helped to put the project team into the mind of the client and helped to guide the way they worked to develop the deliverables, enabling them to ask themselves key questions, and even renegotiate when some of these criteria proved impossible. All in all, developing this 'shopping-list' lowered the inevitable client stress-levels involved in commissioning a politically-sensitive project. This somewhat impressionistic project shopping-list was subsequently reinterpreted into specific outputs, and helped to define some questions that had to be answered. Working in this way, they got to develop their thinking not just about what they wanted, but what it would look like and what it was meant to do.

5 REVERSE/INVERT THE PROBLEM

Sometimes, by inverting or reversing the logic of the situation, you can transform the problem from one you cannot solve, into the one you can.

> In 1843, Isambard Kingdom Brunel, the famous engineer, accidentally swallowed a half-sovereign which remained trapped in his windpipe virtually choking him to death. The attempt to fish the coin out with a specially-designed pair of forceps, through an incision in his throat, failed. Brunel decided to change the nature of the problem: from how to remove the sovereign from Brunel to how to get the sovereign to leave of its own accord. He indicated that he wanted to be strapped to a mirror that was horizontally hinged across its middle and rotated quickly until the coin moved. After several attempts accompanied by coughing fits, the sovereign fell out of his mouth.

The most interesting use of this idea I have come across was when I was asked to work on a staff attitude survey in a leading automotive manufacturer. The key issue was one of high absenteeism. We spent a lot of time constructing a model of absenteeism which grew so large and involved that it covered several walls and was ultimately so dense that we could neither use nor reduce it. The way out was to change the question from 'Why are people absent or what makes them absent from work?' to 'Why do people come to work?', 'Who always comes to work' and 'What motivates them?'

Another example which can pay off is to reverse your role. If you are a leader of a team it is easy to become the 'supplier' of the team's needs, which can mean you have to do everything for them. A way out of this, and of developing a more mature team is to become the team's customer: this means they try to give you what you (as leader) need, which frees you up to do your job and they get to do theirs.

You may find it useful to look back at the H2 Study 3 (see p. 46), where the factory-manager revolutionized the situation of unpredictable product by using his relationship with his suppliers to make it their problem.

Stage 2

GATHER DATA

❖

T his stage of the process can be the most frustrating if we face a truly open problem. We confront the stress-gap head on; and we experience all the pressure to reduce that gap by throwing our old repertoire at the problem.

People sometimes feel that to differentiate between gathering and analysing data involves a false distinction: I disagree. Unless we deliberately separate the gathering from the analysis, we will tend to gather only the data which supports our unstated, implicit picture of the reality we imagine surrounds the problem. In other words, we tend to collect the data which we think will fit.

One of the lessons I learned from working with Japanese engineers was to distinguish between understanding their approach to making products and actually doing it. One morning, we accompanied a small team of these engineers about the shopfloor, orientating them to the manufacturing process and its present level of development. As we worked along the manufacturing process, I was struck by their requirement for measurements and data. Wherever they went, they asked the managers and supervisors for data, a request which usually was not fulfilled. Toward the end of the orientation tour the team approached a workstation and asked the supervisor for the data he used to run that key part of the manufacturing process. Again, this supervisor had none. The team then asked, 'If you don't have data, how can you understand the process?' The response was that since he had been doing this work for fifteen years, he knew the process backwards and didn't need to collect data on it.

Very quietly, but with a good nature that belied the message, the team leader pointed out that without data you know nothing, you possess only opinions. Ultimately if you don't collect the data on the process, you don't control the process – the process controls you.

In another industrial setting, management had developed a team of six shopfloor workers to gather data on the manufacturing process with an eye to truly understanding it in terms of inputs, outputs and opportunities for improvement. Within three months of working as the process-management team, four of the team asked to return to working on the line with their former line colleagues. The training had been expensive and we asked for their reasons. After some hesitation, they admitted it was because their colleagues on the line didn't believe that what they were doing (gathering data) was real work. Fortunately, the team had a 'hit' when it identified three savings which would add up to £150 000 over the next six months. Broadcasting this success revived morale and everyone felt they could look their former colleagues in the eye again.

Gathering data *is* work.

1 PROBLEM-MAPPING

Problem-mapping is a technique for making notes by drawing up a cre-ative 'model' of a topic or subject. The technique works out of our existing mental structures and hangs new information on old frameworks.

There are at least three different ways of describing communication:

Shift	The movement of a pattern to a new location
Slop	The presentation of a mess to someone in the expecta-tion that they will make some sense out of it
Trigger	When all that is passed is a single trigger which unlocks a complete pattern in the receiver

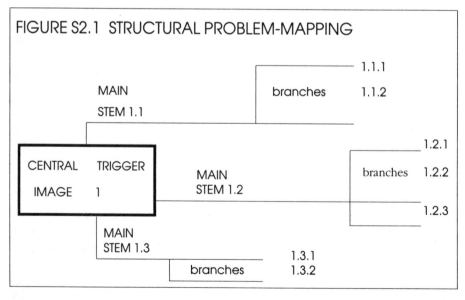

FIGURE S2.1 STRUCTURAL PROBLEM-MAPPING

STRUCTURAL PROBLEM-MAPPING LOGIC

Problem-mapping works by converting a confused communication into a collection of triggers, which can then be transferred to a new location. In effect, problem-mapping is the structuring of information into a layered series of triggers. Once you have the first, central trigger (usually a visual image), you can recall the sub-triggers (through colours, topic-headings and imagery), and in turn you can recall the branches off these main stems. As with Buzan's (1982) mindmapping, knowledge is organized in terms of internal relevance for the recording individual.

Key steps for problem-mapping are:

1   Begin with a strong central image
2   Draw the first main stem at 2 o'clock to the central image
3   Begin each main stem or leg, with a TITLE in capitals and a new colour
4   Develop each branch or spur using lower-case letters
5   Use imagery to aid recall
6   Review and redraft, improving mindmap by saying: 'so what?' and looking for gaps.

Problem-mapping can be a useful way of structuring the output from brainstorming sessions, so that participants can identify the main themes.

Problem-mapping can have unintended effects and gives us some insight into how our minds work to store data. I find that when I come to review my 'maps' of meetings, I can actually smell the room, and if I close my eyes I can work out where I sat, how I felt, what time of day it was and even chunks of dialogue! This visual structure allows us to duplicate much of the original data by recalling the structure on which to hang it.

I began to realize that this was how my mind worked when watching episodes of the TV comedy series *Blackadder*. I noticed that I approximately recalled large chunks of dialogue, but accurately reproduced only short, key ironic phrases that completed a scene. Somewhere in my mind was a structure based on the plot and roughly what had to be said when, with only the denouement embedded in my active memory.

2 TALLY-SHEETS

Tally-sheets or tick-sheets are the basis of observational data in analysing a process, or developing a theory based on facts. If you don't get this right, then everything else you do will be wrong. The tally-sheet is a matrix which uses columns to tell you where something happens and what kind of problems are occurring; and rows to define when they happened.

FIGURE S2.2 AN EXAMPLE OF A TALLY-SHEET

	A	B	C
JANUARY	III	II	I
FEBRUARY	IIII		IIII II
MARCH	I	III	IIII
APRIL	IIII	IIII	IIII III
	14	9	20

A = Telephone call-handling unsatisfactory
B = Slow response to request for repair
C = Unsatisfactory repair

The necessary key is consistency: the classification of events to be recorded must be clearly defined, understood and tested, especially if you use people to collect the data. A pilot to develop your system is very useful. In order to motivate them, the people helping you must share the same understanding of why the data is being gathered, but care must be taken not to influence them toward giving you the data they think will make you happy!

3 MODELS AND THINKING ABOUT PROBLEMS AS SYSTEMS

Edward de Bono described a model as 'a method of transferring some relationship or process from its actual setting to where it is more conveniently studied'. (*The Mechanism of Mind*, 1981.)

A system is a purposeful, organized, connected assembly of components, which are affected by being in the system such that the system's performance is changed if they leave. This assembly has been identified by someone who is interested in it.

Modelling or creating a systemic representation of a problem with all its elements and their relationships is an important part of creative problem-solving and understanding.

A crime-prevention study conducted between 1986 and 1989 on a Rochdale council estate led to a 75 per cent decline in burglaries. In the early 1980s

Kirkholt estate was in decline, with up to 30 per cent unemployment. The estate was run-down and vandalized, with hundreds of empty houses and a burglary in one in four houses. Research discovered that sites of burglary were twice as likely to be burgled again. The project involved the Police, Housing Department, Probation Service, Victim Support Group and criminology experts from Manchester University plus one extra social component: the burglars themselves. By thinking about the problem as a collection of problems existing within a system, identifying all the components and studying their relationships, it became possible to transform the situation.

Part of the 'solution' was to remove the motivation for theft by removing electricity and gas cash meters and coding property; the security of traditional points of burglar entry (doors and windows) was enhanced through simple locks, supported by a neighbourhood watch scheme. But most interesting of all was the inclusion of the local burglars who were themselves involved in explaining their method and reasons for breaking into homes.

That this is nothing new can be seen in the Prussian Army's systemic modelling of war logistics and decision-making upon chess principles (Von Reisswitz's 1824 manual' 'Instructions for the Representation of Tactical Manoeuvres Under the Guise of a War Game', see Dupuy, 1977).

Modelling is a means of exercising our faculty for intense concentration upon a situation or problem, and then directing our attention upon it, combining some elements of creative play.

A company made a model of its level of integration, from customers' demands, through its manufacturing process, to delivery in terms of its product processes and functional departments using coloured beads connected by plastic tubes.

At a second meeting, as the team entered the project-room, the model was brushed onto the floor, turning to its side and breaking in two. The team gathered round the broken model in silence. From this fortuitous accident the team realized that the company's problem was that it was really two separate operations within the same plant. The subsidiary operation was sold off. But for the accident, the team would never have come to such a conclusion.

An often overlooked and ignored aspect of creativity through modelling is what might be called the accidental 'kinaesthetic' effect. In other words, as the above example suggested, the physical manipulation of problem components within a model or arrangement can have dramatic and unpredictable results, especially when you consider that accidental arrangements can radically transform our mindsets by offering what are truly new, and unpredictable compositions of problem components.

OPEN SYSTEMS MODELLING

An open system is one which interacts with its environment, exchanging energy, information or materials across a permeable boundary. Open systems modelling provides a useful level of abstraction from which we can continue the idea of modelling so that we can understand an organization's relationships internally, and across the boundary into its environment: its main points of entry and exit, inputs, transforming processes and outputs, key players, decision-points, decision-making units, its controllable and uncontrollable variables. Thinking about problems as being within open systems helps us to identify the levers and fulcra needed to manage change and predict consequences.

4 ACTIVE DATABASE TECHNIQUE

It is useful to begin a project with a database that is visible, accessible, and allows you to drive your pursuit of information and relationships, to generate iteratively yet further questions, and to keep track of the resulting answers.

In essence, all you need to do is to brainstorm the main data-headings, then use flipcharts with these main headings to list the data summarizing it at team updates on progress and generating, in turn, yet further questions.

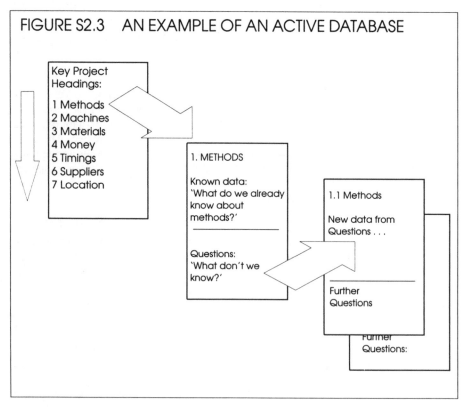

FIGURE S2.3   AN EXAMPLE OF AN ACTIVE DATABASE

This approach makes it possible to expand the database, and delegate questions to sub-teams, managing any programme that requires concurrent data-gathering at a strategic level .

I recommend the use of a laptop computer to save the data as it is recorded onto the flipcharts that you work from, since these may proliferate to provide a fire-hazard!

5 COMPETITIVE BENCHMARKING

If you require data about your problems, go and find someone who has been solving similar problems for longer than you and examine their techniques for dealing with the same problems.

As a technique, it sounds easy. The Japanese are quite happy to host industrial visits because they probably believe that the West will always tend to grasp only the external characteristics of their manufacturing success, by purchasing techniques and ignoring the cultural foundation which drives and make it a reality.

The concept of 'world-class manufacturing' embodies this idea of competitive benchmarking. 'World class' means deliberately deciding to be better than almost every other company in your industry in at least one important aspect of manufacturing. In other words, that you select an area for competitive advantage, prioritizing suitable performance criteria in terms of, for example, cost, quality, dependability, flexibility or innovation, then configure yourself as an organization to achieve and continually enhance that competitive advantage, or until you decide to adopt a new one.

While I suggested the use of a company similar to your own, the deliberate choice of models outside your own area or areas of competition can also be very stimulating because they may have solved similar problems in ways that have never occurred to you.

Competitive benchmarking is a powerful technique for breaking institutional mindsets which support the idea that nothing can be done.

6 PILOT

Sometimes imagination and literary research are not enough and the only way to gather useful hard data is to pilot a process on a small scale. The key to a successful pilot project is to learn as much as possible, with the least possible expense of time, money and effort. The great advantage of a pilot is that it enables you to identify problems, improving your work process before you begin your implementation by raising your learning-curve.

When carrying out commercial research with a new team, I make a point of combining the pilot with competitive benchmarking to provide a solid impartial business perspective of the problem outside the organization, to design the research process and build the team to deliver the project.

7 INTERVIEWING

Interviewing can be effective if you know what you want, and plan to get it. The essential technique is to ask open questions (ones which cannot be answered with a simple yes or no). It can be a good idea to interview in pairs so that your colleague can capture the answers, and generate more questions; or have a single interviewer with an observer who shadows the interviewer to grasp points of finer detail.

Some open questions are:

○ in what way ... ?
○ tell me more about ... ?
○ give me an example of ... ?
○ describe the problems involved in ...
○ how would you make that work?
○ why is it important?

When you need to gather relatively 'soft' data (largely qualitative as opposed to quantitative) or at the beginning of designing a questionnaire to use in an organization, you may wish to consider doing the following:

❖ Plan the structure of the interview (a mindmap may be useful).

❖ Explain the purpose and process of the interview to the subject, and when it will end.

❖ Put up a flipchart displaying the key interview topics, enabling everyone (including the subject) to heighten their attention. Use a piece of Blu-tack to move through the topics, giving a sense of progress.

❖ Encourage the subject to draw or represent answers diagrammatically upon a blank flipchart.

❖ Summarize each topic, checking your understanding of what the subject has said.

❖ Give and ask for feedback. It may be useful to ask whether in the opinion of the subject, you have missed something, and whether they know someone who can give you the data you require.

❖   Review the material as soon as possible after the interview, pro-
        cessing it into summary and arranging triangulation (checking)
        interviews if you feel they are necessary while people are still
        interested in the topic.

8 SUBJECT PROBLEM-MAPPING

This is a team approach to capturing the world that supports and
surrounds the problem, combining elements of interviewing, problem-
mapping, and the active database technique. The accent is upon speed
and building up a problem-map of how the problem is perceived by
someone (the subject) in four steps with a minimal team of three (A, B,
and C).

Figure S2.4 summarizes the technique and gives a bird's-eye view of how
to organize the layout of the room and the relative positions of the team.

The procedure requires the leader or lead researcher (A) to draw a
problem-map as the subject describes the problem. Simultaneously, B and
C listen and draft questions. The subject is encouraged to improve the
problem-map and thus take some ownership of the map. B and C ask
their questions, striking them off as they are answered, while A improves
the map accordingly. When the map is complete, you may want the

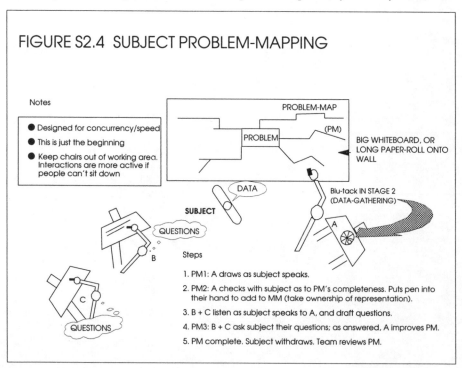

FIGURE S2.4 SUBJECT PROBLEM-MAPPING

Notes

● Designed for concurrency/speed

● This is just the beginning

● Keep chairs out of working area. Interactions are more active if people can't sit down

PROBLEM-MAP

(PM)

PROBLEM

BIG WHITEBOARD, OR LONG PAPER-ROLL ONTO WALL

DATA

Blu-tack IN STAGE 2 (DATA-GATHERING)

SUBJECT

QUESTIONS

A

B

QUESTIONS

C

Steps

1. PM1: A draws as subject speaks.

2. PM2: A checks with subject as to PM's completeness. Puts pen into their hand to add to MM (take ownership of representation).

3. B + C listen as subject speaks to A, and draft questions.

4. PM3: B + C ask subject their questions; as answered, A improves PM.

5. PM complete. Subject withdraws. Team reviews PM.

subject to withdraw while the team jointly review the map. Sometimes the subject or problem-owner is entranced by the way the problem has been drawn or mapped, and becomes very enthusiastic: this may be the first time that they have truly 'seen' the problem from a detached perspective.

You may find yourself overwhelmed by the detail and some creative silence may be useful to help the team review the problem-map and what it ultimately means.

Stage 3

ANALYSE DATA

❖

The analysis of data can be ambiguous if the basis of the investigation is skewed toward supporting a particular point of view. Thus the same combat statistics recorded for the fighting in South Vietnam in 1966 could appear to demonstrate both successful attrition of the Viet-Cong and North Vietnamese through a growing body-count, and Viet-Cong and North Vietnamese managing to maintain the military initiative, by virtue of the fact that they initiated 80 per cent of the combats.

Similarly,

> A manufacturing company's Director of Quality assumed that the process of understanding his manufacturing process was working because the collected data was processed through a customized spreadsheet system into bar-charts, Pareto diagrams, histograms and pie-charts. No analysis was being carried out: he assumed that arranging the data was all that was necessary. For four years, no one had reviewed the data and said 'so what?'.

The process of gathering and arranging data does not itself create information or meaning. Try to be aware of your prejudices. We all tend to see the problem we want to see.

1 FORCE-FIELD ANALYSIS

WHAT IS IT?

Force-field analysis is a method for clarifying the dynamics of a situation by treating it as a system, identifying key elements within the situation and by working on them, making it possible to introduce change or movement into the situation. It is a method which identifies points of leverage and prioritizes change.

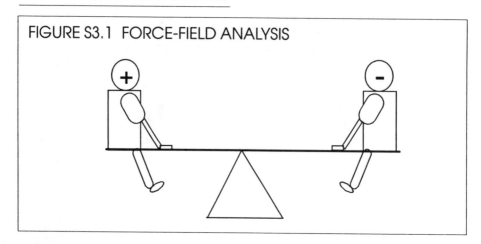

FIGURE S3.1 FORCE-FIELD ANALYSIS

HOW DOES IT WORK?

Force-field analysis assumes that the *status quo* is like a balanced see-saw, that is in a state of equilibrium where both the driving (positive) forces are balanced by restraining (negative) forces (see Figure S3.1). By identifying and measuring the balanced forces we can develop a prioritized plan of action.

The plan should reduce the forces of resistance, which will otherwise tend to grow to compensate for the increased driving force.

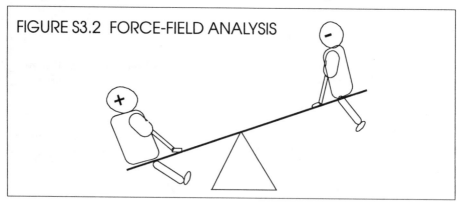

FIGURE S3.2 FORCE-FIELD ANALYSIS

An everyday example might occur on a winter evening when you wish to move a large dog away from the fireplace where there is a blazing log-fire. If you try to push it away, it resists. But if you offer it food, it will move voluntarily.

WHEN SHOULD YOU APPLY FORCE-FIELD ANALYSIS?

When you want to understand the relative strength of the forces working both for and against you, to target the obstacles which you must plan to overcome.

WHAT DO YOU DO?

Step 1: Consider these questions

Where are we now?   Where do we want to be?

X————————————>O

Do we really want to change?
Does it matter if we do nothing?
Who will benefit from a change?

Step 2: Identify all balancing forces

Brainstorm all the forces, then categorize them into positive (driving) or negative (resisting).

FIGURE S3.3 DRIVING AND RESISTING FORCES

Where we are now:	Where we want to be:
34% labour turnover	*2.5% natural labour turnover*
Driving Forces (+)	**Resisting Forces (–)**
D1/New recruits initially well-motivated	R1/Manager promoted above his real level
D2/New profit-share scheme for all workers	R2/Staff training poor: not taken seriously, supervisors used to doing key work themselves
D3/Crèche facilities for working parents	R3/Ineffective office systems: each department has own way of documenting and storing work
D4/High demand for product means buoyant market	R4/Cramped office-space
D5/New partner has injected cash to fund reorganization of systems to respond to new demand for product	R5/Low basic wages mean living wage made through overtime

Step 3: Evaluate the forces and target obstacles

Review the forces by scoring, using different-coloured pens, in terms of 'ease' and 'effect' (ease of implementation, effect: impact on the situation if changed).

Scoring System

FIGURE S3.4 EASE AND EFFECT SCORING

Ease	
1	Cannot be changed

Effect	
1	No impact

2	Could be changed with some investment in resources
3	Easily changed, under your control

2	Some impact
3	High impact

By scoring and totalling the highest scores, we can identify the best levers for introducing change into the situation.

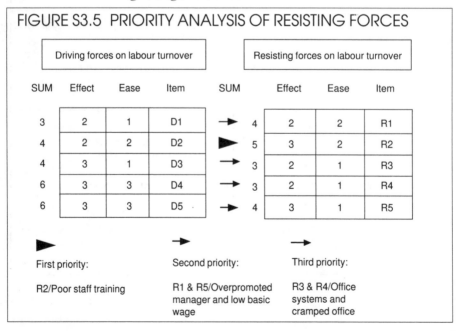

FIGURE S3.5 PRIORITY ANALYSIS OF RESISTING FORCES

Driving forces on labour turnover					Resisting forces on labour turnover			
SUM	Effect	Ease	Item		SUM	Effect	Ease	Item
3	2	1	D1	→	4	2	2	R1
4	2	2	D2	►	5	3	2	R2
4	3	1	D3	→	3	2	1	R3
6	3	3	D4	→	3	2	1	R4
6	3	3	D5	→	4	3	1	R5

►   First priority:

R2/Poor staff training

→   Second priority:

R1 & R5/Overpromoted manager and low basic wage

→   Third priority:

R3 & R4/Office systems and cramped office

As you can see, the 1–3 scoring system doesn't really help to differentiate the forces sufficiently, perhaps a 0–3 system would be more useful. Note that the force-field, while helping to develop an understanding of the situation, is really biased toward developing an implementation strategy leading to a goal or vision.

2 ISHIKAWA DIAGRAM

The Ishikawa diagram is also known as the Fishbone Technique, Xmas Tree or the Cause-and-Effect Diagram. The Ishikawa diagram is a systematic technique for identifying the possible root causes of problems over a period of time. It should be applied when you want to identify the potential contributory causes of a situation, prior to planning, to remove the most powerful causes of the situation.

Using the idea that the best way of understanding a problem is to break it down into its components, the diagram arranges these components in such a way that you can understand how they relate and work together, and then channel your activity to neutralize and overcome the problem.

It is similar to problem-mapping in that it develops a spatial arrangement of the problem components based upon a central point of focus. Instead of generating its own shape *around* a central image, it places the problem or 'effect' in a box where a fish's head might be towards the right-hand side of the page, and links potential causes contributing to the effect, to the left along a fish-spine.

STAGE 1: THE HEAD AND BACKBONE

Be absolutely clear about the 'effect' or problem you wish to overcome. Name the problem or the 'effect', put it into a box on the right-hand side of the flipchart. Draw a horizontal arrow from the left-hand side to the 'effect' box.

STAGE 2: SPECIFY ALL THE PARTS OF THE FISH

Brainstorm all the minor causes, all the components which together constitute the body of the fish onto Post-its (one Post-it per item).

STAGE 3: BUILD THE FISH

Review the problem components (causes), arranging the Post-its into natural family groupings and labelling these major spines of the backbone.

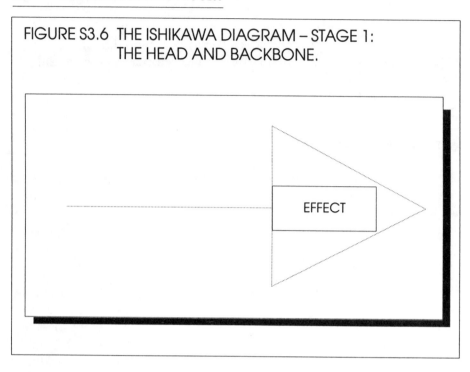

FIGURE S3.6 THE ISHIKAWA DIAGRAM – STAGE 1:
THE HEAD AND BACKBONE.

EFFECT

Alternatively, you may wish to save time by using standard headings, such as the 4M Approach (Methods, Manpower, Machines, Materials), or, PEMPEM: (Plant, Equipment, Materials, People, Environment, Methods).

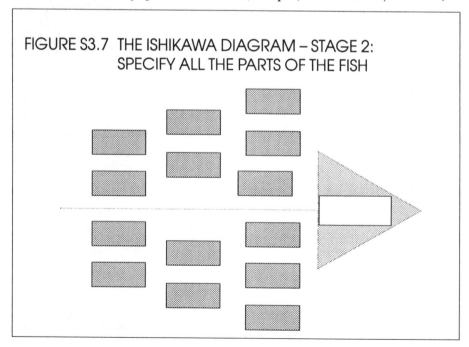

FIGURE S3.7 THE ISHIKAWA DIAGRAM – STAGE 2:
SPECIFY ALL THE PARTS OF THE FISH

STAGE 4: COOKING THE FISH

Continue to build up your fishbone diagram over several sessions and display it. By introducing a period of time to reflect on the diagram, and allowing it to cook itself, the ownership of ideas and blame will recede and the unconscious can help to process the problem.

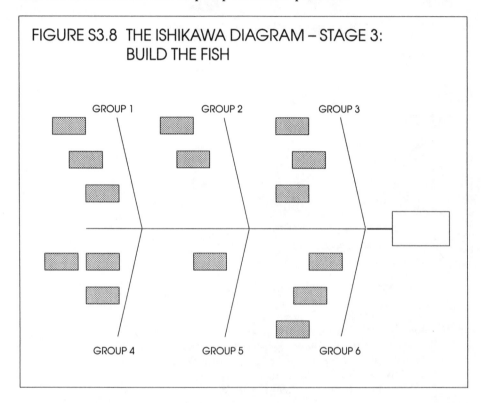

FIGURE S3.8 THE ISHIKAWA DIAGRAM – STAGE 3: BUILD THE FISH

STAGE 5: SERVING AND EATING THE FISH

When the diagram has been fully developed, the group needs to categorize and prioritize areas in terms of importance or complexity for consideration in generating solutions. A relatively fast approach is to review the components in terms of 'ease and effect', using the scoring to prioritize a list of problems.

Another approach is to put all the causes onto pink Post-its on the left-hand side of the labelled spines coming off the backbone, then brainstorm minor solutions onto blue Post-its, putting them to the right of the spine: balancing the minor causes with minor solutions (Figure S3.9). These in turn can be prioritized roughly through locating the blue minor-solution Post-its within an ease and effect matrix (see Stage 5: Select the solution).

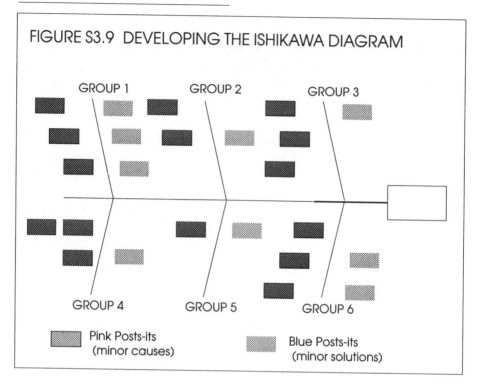

FIGURE S3.9 DEVELOPING THE ISHIKAWA DIAGRAM

At the Sony plant at Bridgend, each team within the manufacturing plant has their own Ishikawa chart on display in its area. Workers put minor causes on red stickers on the left-hand side of the major cause spine, and when someone thinks of a solution to that cause, they balance that minor cause by specifying a solution on a blue sticker on the other, right-hand side of the spine. It is said that most solutions come from workers in the other areas of the plant, who walk past and read each others' Ishikawa charts. This approach leads to constant, visible incremental improvement in the manufacturing process.

3 WHY/WHY DIAGRAMS

Why/Why diagrams serve the same purpose as the Ishikawa/Fishbone/ cause and effect approach. Why/Why builds a structure out of an effect or problem-statement and generates a pyramid of causes and sub-causes by continually asking the question 'Why?' until you find that you either run out of answers or the same answers keep coming up. Why/Why is very useful in tracking down the systemic nature of a problem.

What is not shown in the Why/Why diagram depicted in Figure S3.10 is the original messiness of the first version. In reality you would discover connections from one line of causes to another, and you would connect these with either a coding system, or visually with a piece of coloured string from connected Post-it cause to Post-it cause.

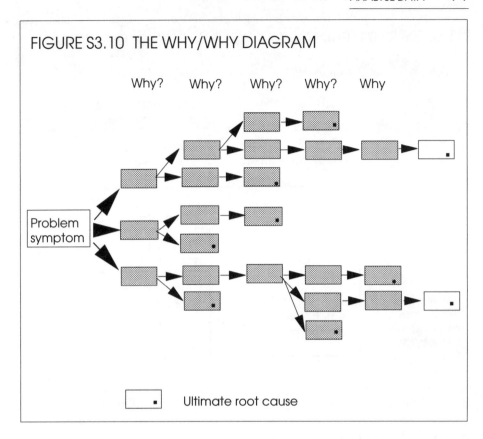

FIGURE S3.10 THE WHY/WHY DIAGRAM

The Why/Why diagram in Figure S3.10 is an extract from a much larger and involved diagram developed out of a joint management/union lean production implementation programme workshop. We began by asking both groups the same question about the failure of the last three continuous improvement programmes, then integrated their answers into a single diagram to present a total picture from both unions and management.

I find Why/Why diagrams very useful for exploring blocks in how people see the problems. When they cannot answer the Why? question any further and show exasperation this often betrays a mindset about the issue which needs exploration and challenge.

4 INFLUENCE DIAGRAMS

Influence diagrams are linked to Ishikawa and and Why/Why but different in that they attempt to arrange the components of the problem into a causal flow of events connected by arrows.

Apart from mapping the problem, the idea is to identify cycles which are vicious and reinforcing, and rebuild them or replace them with virtuous, reinforcing ones.

FIGURE S3.11 PART OF A LARGER WHY/WHY DIAGRAM

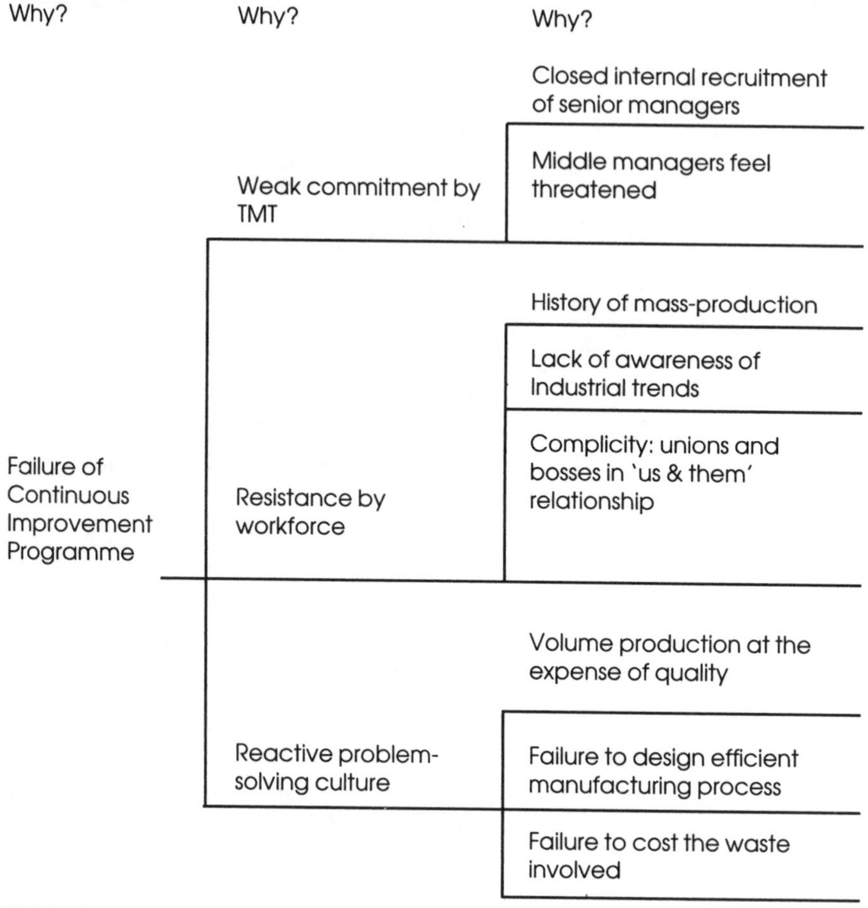

Why?	Why?	Why?
Failure of Continuous Improvement Programme	Weak commitment by TMT	Closed internal recruitment of senior managers
		Middle managers feel threatened
	Resistance by workforce	History of mass-production
		Lack of awareness of Industrial trends
		Complicity: unions and bosses in 'us & them' relationship
	Reactive problem-solving culture	Volume production at the expense of quality
		Failure to design efficient manufacturing process
		Failure to cost the waste involved

In Figure S3.12, you can see the way in which a client's deliberate pursuit of product sales volume has created chaos within the company: in the form of financial, administrative and production schedule chaos, which requires even greater pursuit of volume in order to maintain cash-flow and pay the price for the daily chaos they themselves are engineering into their manufacturing system through their sales policy.

In Figure S3.13, we can see the parallel, vicious pricing cycle which mutually reinforces an uncritical pursuit of volume cycle, both combining to destabilize the ability to manage the manufacturing process. The assumption seems to be that the manufacturing operation has unlimited capacity, that customers will not learn to go to another manufacturer as a result of delivery and service failures. The basic business mindset is virtually that of a monopoly or a cost-plus manufacturer, where the sales and

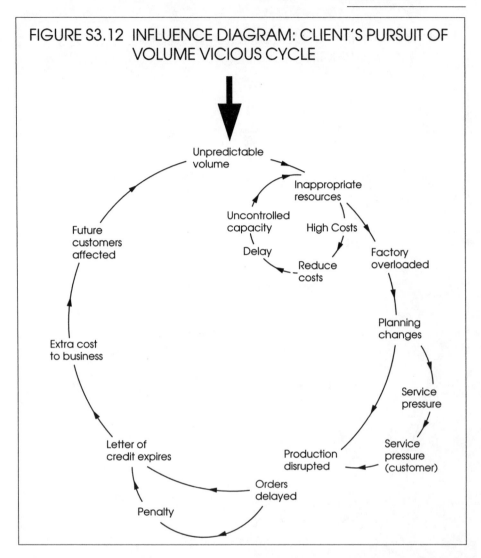

FIGURE S3.12 INFLUENCE DIAGRAM: CLIENT'S PURSUIT OF
VOLUME VICIOUS CYCLE

manufacturing arms have no feedback loops and operate without either
a profit or cost-model to direct their activities into some kind of joint syn-
ergy.

In Figure S3.14, we can represent an influence diagram based upon the
idea of introducing stability through linking actual manufacturing volume
to profit targets by introducing an explicit relationship between volume
and profit through a prioritization system linking cost of manufacture and
delivery to price and potential profit.

Influence diagrams are a way of capturing and displaying the vicious
cycle of reinforcing behaviours which are present in an organization's
way of either running themselves or behaving. Once the influence dia-

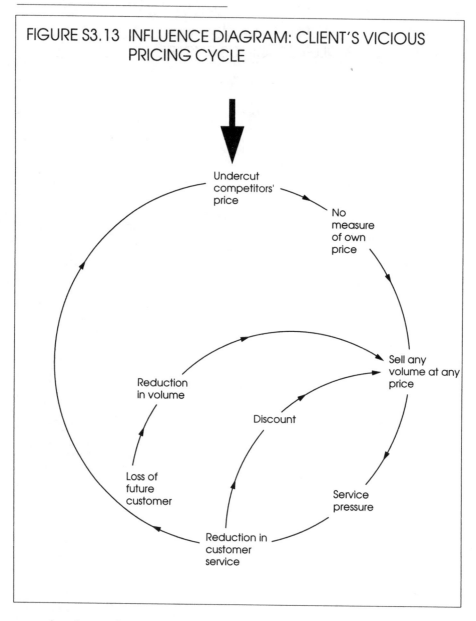

FIGURE S3.13 INFLUENCE DIAGRAM: CLIENT'S VICIOUS PRICING CYCLE

gram has been drawn and accepted as a fair representation, it offers an excellent opportunity to begin the process of designing the virtuous cycle which could replace it.

I have often found the moment of recognition on the part of participants, of even partial and incomplete influence diagrams to be almost magical. It is as though once people can see their reality and how it is engineered in one piece, and not just as a collection of cynical stories, it becomes possible to confront and overcome it.

Developing and drawing up influence diagrams requires some serious reflection and a willingness to play with the components of the crisis. Influence diagrams can make novel connections which may not be initially apparent to participants, based upon sound foundations of consistent interviewing to gather the data and make the connections.

If you can start a Why/Why diagram with a good central question or issue, it becomes possible to translate it into an influence diagram through transposing the Post-its by which you originally built up the Why/Why diagram.

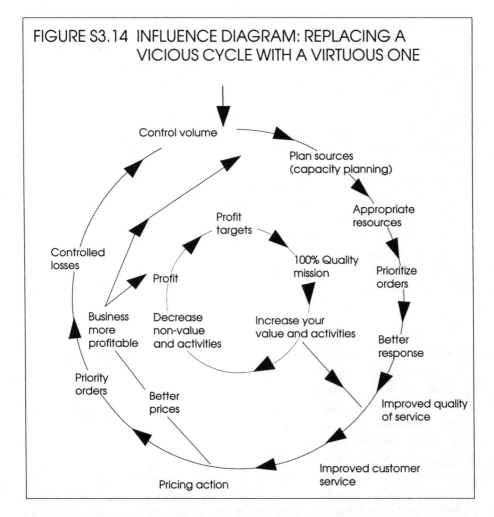

FIGURE S3.14 INFLUENCE DIAGRAM: REPLACING A VICIOUS CYCLE WITH A VIRTUOUS ONE

THE FOUR TECHNIQUES REVIEWED

All four techniques described in this section require some shared, if only partial understanding of the problem at the outset. Once one technique is introduced, you begin to develop a structure, based on mapping, for what are in effect, causes of the problem.

I believe that the way these techniques are introduced in books and workshops, that is, with an implicit message of tidiness, keeps them at the level of clever ideas which though understood are rarely used. All four are the better for being constructed with coloured Post-its, introducing the possibility of movement. *All four techniques exist to link symptoms with systems, effects with process.* The key is for us to capture a symptom to begin what is after all, a form of guided discussion to discover the body of the system or the process that delivers the effect we wish to remove or shift.

It is only when you begin to map the system or process that you find that each person involved has a *different* view of the same system and the symptom, which means that although both of you may use the same words, you mean something different, and experience the problem according to where you see it or where it impacts you.

The mapping process, whether in the form of listing apparently dichotomous driving or resisting forces, or the mapping of components through relationships captures only an impression of reality. Unless we are prepared to move into testing relationships through coefficients, the map or diagram only represents an impression of the problem.

The key to the success of the techniques is the nature of the guided discussion that helps us to link different perspectives and mindsets together to draw a problem-map where we develop a shared understanding of the problem, and slow down our tendency to jump into solutions out of our standing repertoire.

FORCE-FIELD

The implicit purpose of changing the situation we are looking at, tends to pre-empt any real diagnostic nature to this approach. I know of change consultants who use virtually no other technique, but again, they are in the business of shifting a business, and where he who hesitates can be accused of wasting time.

Its weakness lies in the way it operates in the shadow of an implicit solution. After all, it is hard to define the opposing forces that preserve the present balanced situation without the contrast of knowing in some way what the solution is going to look like. **Force-field tells us more about what prevents us having what we want than why the situation has occurred.**

ISHIKAWA/FISHBONE

The Ishikawa has been a favourite technique because of the kinaesthetic aspect of accidental creativity through play that coloured Post-its allowed: developing the body of the fish, structuring it, then moving unselfconsciously into solutions which can then be prioritized through the ease and effect matrix. **Fishbone maps our perception of what collectively makes the problem happen.**

WHY/WHY

Why/Why seems to reveal the nature of the mindset and allow it to be mapped without confrontation. Developing the structure, through asking the question 'Why' offers no easy answers but the resulting layers of 'Why' begin to form a pyramid-structure that has fallen onto its side, so that instead of only the original symptom peaking above the surface, we see the whole thing.

Whenever I discover an issue where the problem-owner can go no further, I 'bullet' the Post-it with a cannon-ball dot, and move to another area of the structure. Like all the techniques, we can re-shuffle the structure like a problem-map to make it tidy and create clearer linkages.

Later, you can return to the bulleted 'no-go areas' that demarcate the boundaries of the mindset, and pick them off, one by one.

As with fishbones, it is easy to move into How/How, working from the widest extent of the pyramid-base, back up to original symptom and thus demolish it. **Why/Why maps the problem and contours the boundaries of our mindsets.**

INFLUENCE DIAGRAMS

Influence diagrams penetrate deeper than the first three techniques, to map the *logic* of the systems that create the symptom, which is not the same as mapping the causes. The difference is that the influence diagram attempts to tell you 'how' the symptom is manufactured, not just why. **Influence diagrams capture the reinforcing, logical loops within the sub-systems of the situation that act together to deliver their unintended effects upon the environment.**

Stage 4

GENERATE SOLUTIONS

1 TRADITIONAL BRAINSTORMING

There is probably no other problem-solving technique so widely used nor so incompetently applied, as brainstorming.

At its simplest, the technique is a meeting for up to 12 people, conducted under special rules designed to delay the judgement of individuals' ideas as they appear, to a later stage. Brainstorming sessions can be active and noisy, often requiring two people to capture all the ideas as they are voiced, onto flipcharts.

Do not begin a brainstorming session without defining the problem to your own satisfaction in the form of an agreed problem-statement based on a review of all the data.

Brainstorming can be conducted in waves, each wave of ideas generated acting as 'triggers' for individuals to generate yet further ideas in succeeding waves. The first wave is the most important and will tend to determine the shape of later waves of ideas.

Brainstorming is best applied to 'open' problems, when you genuinely want new ideas or solutions, and not for 'closed' problems, that is problems with only one solution or outside the control of the participants.

PLANNING A BRAINSTORMING SESSION

When you are preparing for a brainstoming session, you need to ask a few questions first:

> Problem: Is it open or closed?
> How closed is it?

Owner: Whose problem is it really?
Timing: How much time have we got?

Environment

When planning a brainstorming session, you need a location without distractions, prepared blank flipcharts on the walls (blutac or masking-tape, according to surface), and flipchart pens (blue, green, or black: avoid red, brown or yellow).

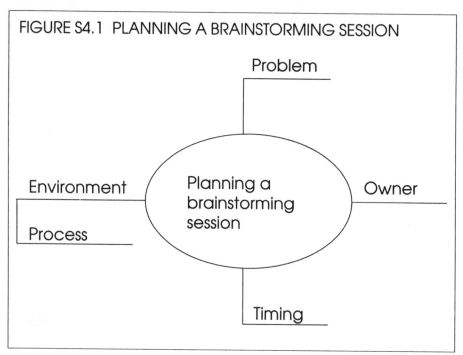

FIGURE S4.1 PLANNING A BRAINSTORMING SESSION

You should also have a flipchart displaying the 'rules' of brainstorming on it, and a semi-circle of not too comfortable chairs facing the flipcharts, with flipchart pens underneath with at least two pads of different-coloured Post-its. If you must have a table, make it small enough for everyone to sit knee-to-knee. Organize diversions such as coffee within the room, or even volleyball or a group walk outside to discuss the ideas so far.

Process

Help direct participants' attention onto the brainstorming process by running a quick warm-up. Look at today's newspaper, and find a topic which people would find interesting and entertaining. Avoid the ubiquitous 'uses of a paperclip', try to find something topical, with a potential owner, like 'preventing car-theft', 'bomb-proofing passenger aircraft', 'how to get value-for-money out of business consultants', or 'a nappy that doesn't need changing'.

LEADING A BRAINSTORMING SESSION

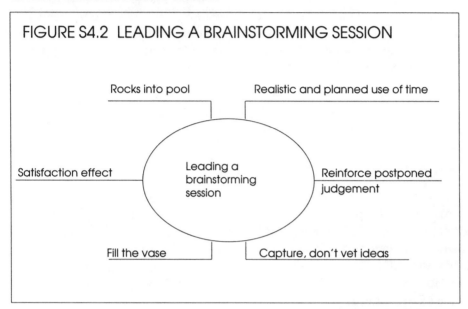

FIGURE S4.2 LEADING A BRAINSTORMING SESSION

Rocks into pool

Realistic and planned use of time

Satisfaction effect

Leading a brainstorming session

Reinforce postponed judgement

Fill the vase

Capture, don't vet ideas

Encourage a team to postpone any judgement of ideas generated and capture these ideas on flipcharts, by

❖ *Realistic and planned use of time.* Participants need to feel confident that you know how much time to allocate to activities. The process leading up to, and following the session needs to make sense and the objective needs to be achievable within the timeframe.

❖ *Reinforcing the need to postpone judgement* (best done in the warm-up through personal feedback). Agree on the recognized use of a visual cue when people break into evaluating ideas, like putting your hand over your mouth.

❖ *Capture, don't vet ideas.* Sometimes you will not actually remember hearing ideas you dislike, or you may find yourself changing the words and ultimately the meaning of an idea in order to save space on the flipchart. Ask individuals to re-phrase, always confirm with individuals that you've got it right. You may have missed the point altogether.

❖ *Helping the team to 'fill the vase'.* Regard the session as a vase which the team fill with their own ideas. If there is a silence: let the team fill it. Don't fill the vase yourself with your own ideas. You can be the most disruptive person in the room.

❖   *Use the 'satisfaction effect'.* You will have to judge this yourself. If you create a false target for the team in terms of volume of ideas or timing, you can plan to exceed these targets. When the lower ideas threshold is achieved, the team relaxes and the quality of ideas radically improves.

❖   *Throwing rocks into the pool.* The team may be digging themselves into a rut. Use a dictionary to introduce random words to disturb the pattern. Become Harpo to everyone's Margaret Dumont!

THE ASSUMPTIONS BEHIND BRAINSTORMING

There are two prevalent assumptions about brainstorming. One is that creative thinking depends upon divergent or lateral thinking. (Divergent or lateral thinking is when a thinker overcomes blocks or existing patterns and structures and allows the unconscious free rein.) The other is that brainstorming eliminates judgement and combination in groups.

However, brainstorming research (Weisberg, 1986: pp. 61–69) suggests, that as a technique

O   group problem-solving is less productive than that of individuals.
O   brainstorming rules are less effective than instructions which emphasize initial criteria and judgement of the problem (that is, make sure you understand what the problem is, before you try to solve it).

2 CREATIVE SILENCE OR BRAINSTORMING II

If group problem-solving is less productive than that of individuals, why use group problem-solving techniques at all? Some consultants have found that generating large numbers of ideas doesn't imply a larger number of potential nuggets. Similarly, the free-association aspect of brainstorming is often more useful as a means of mapping the preoccupations and thinking styles of the participating group than in generating useful ideas.

THE DANGER OF THE FIRST IDEA

Another difficulty is that the first idea voiced, may prove to be the last.

Researchers have found that short stress-gaps in teams, combined with a high need to produce an output can lead to the generation of ideas long before the team has agreed and formally defined a problem. Such teams are easily led astray by the first idea. It is as though the first idea dominates or 'shapes' everything that follows.

The tendency of the first idea shaping what follows can be observed to have quite dramatic effects, especially in outdoor management development courses. I recall a powerful incident where the team had a series of outdoor obstacles to cross and had difficulties in prioritizing and applying the resources available.

> One member of the team quickly modelled the problem, using twigs, gravel and matchsticks. The team stopped their own thinking and concentrated on his model. Naturally, everyone asked him for his idea. He explained. Thereupon, everyone hunkered down, and began to manipulate his model and develop his idea. The stress-levels had visibly diminished, everyone was happy. Ultimately, the team failed to complete the task because they had only generated one basic idea, and all their thinking went into developing variants of that *first* and only idea.

The need to work on something, often anything, means that the *first* idea voiced, slants or directs the ideas that follow. The team 'vets' the initial idea, producing variations and embellishments, investing in this direction until, much too late, it realizes that this area is rather unproductive but feels unwilling to abandon work which has taken so much effort and time.

> I was asked to evaluate the business strategy of a European corporation. I was presented with the corporate strategy and a prototype document proposing how the business strategy was going to deliver the corporate strategy. Neither document explained the problems the strategies were meant to solve, and the solutions were almost exclusively the product of half-understood 'me-too-isms' based upon what they felt the competition were doing.

The solution is to overcome this type of 'groupthink' by introducing a new discipline to traditional brainstorming, by asking individuals to 'kick-off' the process of generating solutions or ideas by doing it individually, in silence. This 'creative silence' approach leads to a significant improvement in quality and diversity or ideas. The resulting ideas are collected by asking individuals to contribute their ideas singly, and without comment, working round the team until all the ideas are represented. This also encourages individuals to listen to each other's ideas to avoid presenting the same idea again.

I find Post-its for individual ideas a very useful way of accelerating this process. I have no investments in the manufacturers, nor do I (as yet) receive a retainer for making this suggestion!

Remember: One idea per Post-it, write all ideas with the same colour flipchart-pen, to disguise the ownership of ideas and reduce status-awareness.

Brainstorming – 5 basic rules	
1	2 minutes creative silence
2	No evaluation during generation
3	The wilder the idea, the better
4	The greater the quantity, the more chance of a winner
5	Seek combination and improvement

Once the first wave of ideas on Post-its has been generated, encourage individuals to introduce their Post-its in their own words, without comment from the team beyond checking their understanding of the necessarily abbreviated content of each Post-it as it is put on display.

While this is happening, encourage individuals to respond to what they see, generating further ideas onto additional Post-its, but holding these back until called for. The next steps can either involve further generation of ideas (another wave) or lead to grouping the ideas into families, identifying gaps and only then introducing another wave through creative silence, and so on.

Remember: groups are very good at spotting gaps between and in, other people's ideas.

TWO TYPES OF IDEAS GENERATED: THE PROBLEMS OF WHAT AND HOW

Sometimes the definition of the problem needs to be relatively open and leads to the generation of ideas that are of two types, dealing with the 'how' of how we will manage the activity to solve the problem (in other words: the process) and the 'what', the technique or tactic we will employ to solve the problem.

The problem	Incoming shifts are unaware of problems with processing machinery experienced by outgoing shifts
The what (do we do about it?)	Record all problems into a shift log-book which is passed onto next shift

The how (do we do it?)	Incoming shift will be briefed as a team by outgoing shift supervisor; to include trends and dangers, any remedial re-settings of machinery; incoming supervisor to initial all items in log-book.

3 DE BONO'S 6 THINKING HATS

Edward de Bono's Thinking Hats technique is a deliberate technique enabling a thinker to choose how to conduct their thinking. Just as you might choose to put on a hat to suit a particular occasion, you can choose to suit your thinking to the situation. The thinker can control their thinking style, choosing to do just one thing at a time: separating emotion from logic, creativity from information, and pessimism from optimism.

Hat-Colour	Visualize	Thinking-Style
WHITE	A sheet of paper with the facts written plainly on it	Objective and dispassionate: 'show me all the facts'
RED	High blood-pressure, see the human cost	Emotions: 'this is how I feel about it'
BLACK	Doom and gloom	It won't work because ...
YELLOW	Sunrise, a new day dawning	Positive: Yes, we can do it!
GREEN	A garden full of beautiful plants no one has ever seen before	Creativity: We can do anything. Dare to think the unthinkable
BLUE	The view of the ground from a helicopter in the sky	Where are we now? where are we going? what are we doing?

The Thinking Hats technique is a useful way of identifying individuals' preferred thinking style, and then deliberately loosening it up. It is suitable for use throughout the problem-solving process. The hats are coloured. The technique links the colour of the hat to a particular thinking style. Once you are familiar with the colour and the style of thinking, you can put on and remove a Thinking Hat according to the situation.

The only weakness in the approach may be the choice of colours. While teams often agree about the thinking styles, they do not consistently identify the styles with de Bono's colours. Also why hats? Why not consider tinted-spectacles, cloaks, gloves, places or even thinking odours?

It may be useful to create a schedule of the colours used by team members to map preferred thinking-styles, encouraging team awareness and a more balanced distribution by the team when solving problems.

4 NOMINAL GROUP TECHNIQUE

The chief advantage of the Nominal Group Technique (NGT) is that it permits the team to meet formally, without restricting independent thinking, as tends to occur through the personal dynamics of an interacting group where status prevents brainstorming.

NGT restricts discussion or interpersonal communication during the decision-making process, hence the term: 'nominal'. Group members are all physically present, as in a traditional committee meeting, but members operate independently. A problem is presented, and then

O   Members meet as a group, but before any discussion takes place, each member independently writes down their ideas on the problem.

O   This silent period is followed by each member presenting one idea to the group. Each member takes their turn going round the table, presenting a single idea until all ideas have been presented and recorded on a flipchart. No discussion takes place until all ideas have been recorded.

O   The group now discusses the ideas for clarity and evaluates them.

O   Each member silently and independently ranks the ideas. The final decision is determined by the idea with the highest aggregate ranking.

A VARIATION: THE 6–3–5 TECHNIQUE

In this variation the group consists of a team of six, where each individual generates three ideas, five times in succession.

Each individual is given three cards and asked to think of three ideas and put each idea on a card. These cards are then passed to other members in succession, each individual reading each card and triggering an additional idea underneath each idea. These ideas in turn stimulate further ideas on the next exchange of cards. These cards can then be put on display, and each team member given a highlighter pen to indicate the ideas they would like to develop.

5 DELPHI TECHNIQUE

A group decision method, the Delphi technique was developed by the Rand Corporation, in which individuals, acting separately, systematically and independently, pool their judgement. This approach is similar, though more complex than the NGT. Group members never meet face-to-face.

○ The problem is identified and members are asked to provide potential solutions through a series of carefully designed questionnaires.

○ Each member independently and anonymously completes the first questionnaire.

○ The results of the first questionnaire are compiled centrally, transcribed, reproduced and sent out to the participants.

○ Participants review the results, and are asked again for their solutions. These results lead to new solutions or a change in the original problem-statement.

○ The last two steps are repeated until consensus is reached.

The Delphi technique has the advantage of facilitating consultation among a geographically disparate population of managers across several continents. The technique is extremely slow, but with the increasing use of faxes and electronic mail systems, may become more useful.

Generally used as a method for forecasting future developments, especially technological discoveries. The approach pools the opinions of experts and calls for

❖ Anonymous prediction of important events in the area in question, from each expert in a group in the form of brief statements. Each may also be asked to comment upon the desirability, feasibility and timing of these developments.

❖ A clarification of these statements by an investigator.

❖ The successive, individual requestioning of each of the experts, combined with feedback supplied from the other experts via the investigator.

In essence, the Delphi technique is a consensus forecasting approach, and accordingly may tell you more about present beliefs than actual future outcomes.

6 'YES, AND . . .'

The 'Yes, and . . .' technique, is a method of overcoming premature dismissal of ideas by accepting the idea and building on it.

When we discuss ideas in a group, it is difficult (except in a well-trained team) to treat ideas dispassionately. It is no exaggeration to refer to ideas as people's 'babies'; and much energy is wasted in protecting these offspring though a mistaken sense of ownership.

Through use of the 'Yes, and . . .' technique, it becomes possible to work with every idea generated, making even what appears to be a crazy idea, ultimately usable.

> 'I have just had the idea of putting heating elements into windscreens so that they will clear faster on frosty, winter mornings.'

Traditional approach:

> 'Yes, **but** in a head-on collision the driver and passengers' faces could be affected by these sharp, wire-like elements travelling at speed, and holding it together like a missile.'

The 'Yes, and ...' technique builds on the idea without dismissing it altogether:

> **'Yes, and ...**
>
> ... we could design it so the elements were further apart.'
>
> ... we could use a type of metallic oxide in the glass, retaining the shatter-ability of the old ones and yet still conduct electricity and heat.'
>
> ... we could find a way to give the ice an opposing charge so that it just slides off.'
>
> ... what about reversing what drivers do in hot climates: those paper-shields behind car-windscreens? Make a permanent wind-on inset windscreen cover which reflected heat, for use in both hot and cold climates?'
>
> ... why not do away with windscreens altogether and use a retracting, heated, wide-angle CCTV camera system with an internal screen viewer like a windscreen, with the advantages of infra-red filters for night driving and poor visibility, reducing the need for streetlighting and ambient atmospheric light pollution?'

These examples may seem exaggerated, but they give an impression both of the spirit of the idea and the opportunity they create for breaking out of mindsets.

7 STRANGE/FAMILIAR: METAPHOR AND ANALOGY

Strange and familiar are the two key-words or mechanisms for creative thinking. They provide us with two choices when we face a problem. When the problem seems strange to us, or unrecognizable, we can reduce its apparent strangeness through confident use of a familiar technique to analyse it. When the problem seems familiar and we are tempted to drop too quickly into a knee-jerk response out of old repertoire, we can deliberately choose to make the problem seem strange by transforming it into something new or different and studying it.

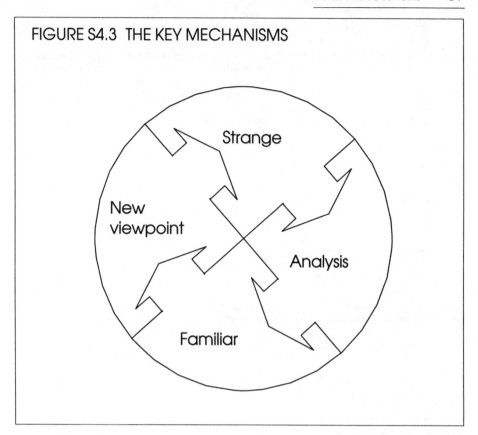

FIGURE S4.3 THE KEY MECHANISMS

THE KEY MECHANISMS

- *Make the strange into something familiar*: This is classic approach to problem-solving – to analyse problems (initially seen as strange), using a familiar process.
- *Making the familiar into something strange:* Deliberately view the problem from an unfamiliar perspective, adopting a new viewpoint which seems to distort the problem.

THE METAPHORICAL MECHANISMS

PERSONAL: Imagine yourself as the problem.

I have known this to be a good 'escape' technique when the emotional aspect of a problem has been the key to its solution. A government body was scheduled for handover to the local authorities. The problem was two-fold: how to manage it properly, and how to maintain morale to the end. The answer was to visualize the government body as a 'gift', not something to be thrown away. And part of giving any gift is to make sure it is something that represents your character and your feeling for the person being given it: if you see it as valuable, then they will, too.

Authors do this all the time when writing autobiography, 'method' actors have been known to take it to extremes. Montgomery kept a picture of Rommel in his caravan to put himself in his enemy's mental shoes.

In the absence of the ability to decode U-boat messages in the early days of signal intelligence, the Royal Navy appointed Rodger Winn, a barrister crippled with polio, to interpret the U-boat strategy from the vestigial data of transmission fixed, volumes and reported sinking. His ability to think himself into the minds of the U-boat commanders and their leaders to understand and imagine their strategy was a powerful weapon in the 1941 War of the Atlantic.

DIRECT: Look for something that solves a similar problem or looks as though it works in the way you want it to.

Brunel's invention of underwater tunnelling caissons through the analogy of a ship-worm tunnelling through timber, constructing a tube for itself as it moved forward.

The discovery that the long loops in kidney tubules were a counter-current multiplier through an engineer recognizing the physical similarity to an existing device for increasing the concentration of solutions.

The idea of the personal telephone that operates independently of a fixed installation, like a walkie-talkie radio: probably influenced by the communicators used in the original Star-Trek series.

From the Dambusters' raid: the idea of the bouncing-bomb based on skipping stones across water, judging exact bomb-release height for low-flying Lancaster bombers at night through fixed lights shone onto the surface of the lake: based on stage spotlights illuminating a singer on an otherwise darkened stage.

SYMBOLIC: Use objective and impersonal images to describe the problem, finding the solution in the symbol.

A car-jack designed to emulate the Indian rope-trick.

Laser weapons-sighting mechanism based on the image of a train of explosives smoothly riding a rail which leads to a target station.

Stealth 'bomber' wearing a cloak which makes it invisible, carrying no bombs, but functioning as a 'torch' distinguishing the target.

FANTASY: How, in our wildest fantasy could the problem be solved? Imagine a super-hero or fantastic creature which can carry out the function you require; try to visualize it operating, solving the problem.

I suspect that the Special Air Service 'Pagoda Troop' that broke the Iranian Embassy Siege in 1981 was heavily influenced by the James Bond Film: *You Only Live Twice*, featuring the anonymous, black-uniformed, Ninja-trained fighters who used special techniques and equipment to approach and enter their target, then fought with tremendous speed and skill to overwhelm the enemy. The parallels are obvious.

You will probably recognize the difficulty of discretely separating these mechanisms.

8 'HOW TO...'

I introduced you to this technique in the first stage of the problem-solving

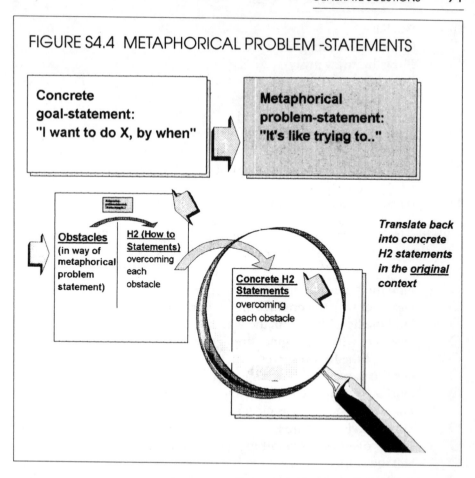

FIGURE S4.4 METAPHORICAL PROBLEM -STATEMENTS

process. 'How to ...' is a useful way of introducing the use of metaphorical thinking by deliberately thinking through metaphors.

Start with an 'I want ...' statement, then transform it into a metaphor by reviewing the 'I want ...' statement and trying to find another way of expressing it as though you were trying to explain the problem to a child: 'The problem is like trying to ...'. Develop obstacles to the new metaphorical problem statement and create 'how to's' within the new, metaphorical context. Following are a few examples of how this technique could work.

I want to find and recover a kidnap victim

'It's like trying to find a needle in a haystack': H2 find a needle in a haystack

O   Make it into a series of smaller haystacks
O   Sieve it

○   Wash it
○   Move it with a magnet
○   Blow the straw away
○   Burn it
○   Encourage people to eat it
○   Tell people it is made of gold
○   Turn it into a competition, offer a prize
○   Surround it with more haystacks
○   Put several gold needles into the same haystack

I want to rescue a declining, directionless business

'It's like trying to salvage a ship adrift on the high seas': H2 to salvage a ship adrift on the high seas

---

○   Find the holes letting in the water
○   Discover why the engines aren't working properly
○   Find the holes letting in the water
○   Discover why the engines aren't working
○   Measure the fuel-reserves
○   Get the passengers working
○   Find out where we're going and why
○   Put out a distress message and get help
○   Find a navigator who knows these waters
○   Throw overboard everything we don't need
○   Sell the ship to the passengers
○   Find the nearest land to our present position
○   Inspect the lifeboats, emergency equipment and rations
○   Allocate leaders to lifeboats

I want to negotiate with the leader of a powerful, sectional interest

---

'It's like trying to cut out the pain you get when you have to bang your head against a brick wall': H2 remove the pain involved in banging your head against a brick wall.

○   Wear a helmet
○   Undermine the wall
○   Replace the bricks with pillows
○   Replace the wall with a hologram
○   Pad the wall
○   Go beyond the wall, so it's behind you

○   Tunnel underneath it

I want to help the managers in a depressed business, trapped within a self-reinforcing spiral of decline.

> 'It's like trying to help the inmates of a PoW camp to escape': H2 help the PoWs escape.

○   Extend the boundaries of the camp until surveillance become impossible
○   Dress up like guards and walk out
○   Sell tickets to enter on guided tours
○   Dig tunnels outside
○   Build a glider
○   Fill the camp with dummies
○   Invite people who prefer life in a PoW camp to enter and stay
○   Make extra huts so that no one can be found

And, finally the issue that I keep facing with businesses who want to reinvest themselves through redesigning their business processes:

I want to transform a staid, old-fashioned business trapped in obsolete technology and products, out of all recognition into a serious, modern competitor within the emerging market.

> 'It's like trying to ...': How to transform an old transport galley that's powered by slaves pulling oars, into a modern, cargo-carrying nuclear submarine, while keeping our contracts with existing customers, not sinking and moving into new routes without making a loss.

These examples are just the beginning of the process. The most interesting part is to go on to the next stage, and convert the ideas from a metaphorical state back to reality in the form of concrete examples that can contribute to solving the original problem.

For example, let's take the kidnap/lost needle metaphor. The metaphorical ideas can be translated into the following ideas:

• Introducing the news of a natural/unnatural disaster or accident which would require the evacuation or inoculation of the population, allowing us to either find the victim in the resulting administration of the movement of population or to search a landscape uncluttered by other people, on the basis that the only person left alive, must be the victim. (This is a combination of: sieve/wash/blow/burn ideas.)

• The extraction of the victim by making the kidnappers eject the victim on the grounds that he or she had a contagious disease, wasn't the real victim but living out a fantasy; or that the real victim was being held by someone else (magnet).

• Mobilization of the population in the area to contribute to the search, motivating them with the knowledge that each 'successful' finding of a 'victim' found additional to the real victim leads them closer to winning a share in the competition; and creates an atmosphere where areas are searched again and again (introducing several gold needles/ encourage people to eat it/ sell the straw as a health-food/ made of gold).

9 VISUALIZATION

Visualization is a technique for developing a picture, or a vision, of what we want. Visualizing helps us to develop direction and anticipation in order to demolish mindsets which suggest there is no alternative approach to the problem as we see it:

Direction:	Know where we want to go
Anticipation:	Plan a route to get there by anticipating and planning to overcome the obstacles

The ability to dream is an important element in motivating individual and groups to make a change.

> After Dunkirk, the British Army had to develop a new way of fighting. Battle Schools were created, designed by young officers without battle experience, who had to learn about Blitzkrieg from the veterans of the Spanish Civil War. These schools had to create new battle-drills and processes to train officers and men to operate in an environment they themselves had never experienced.

Visualizing the future in great detail through a mixture of common sense and imagination to anticipate and simulate your problems, planning and training to solve them, can offer great bonuses.

However, it takes courage to dream in detail. If we look at how managers solve problems, one of the traditional weaknesses is to only solve the *next* problem that appears as opposed to planning to solve a predictable stream of problems through to completion. Visualization is a key technique for building a bridge between the future and where we stand.

> There is a science-fiction story which I can't unfortunately source, set in the early period of the Cold-War. A team of scientists is taken to a top-secret, secure location and shown a clandestine film of a secret device which the enemy is develop-

ing. The inventor is shown controlling what appears to be a form of anti-gravity device. The team is given unlimited resources. Within six months, they surpass the reported performance of the original device. They return to the secure location to celebrate, and are introduced to the 'inventor' in the clandestine film. They have obviously been hoaxed and feel, initially, very angry; but they calm down when the director of the project points out their achievement: they have done something that was originally believed to be impossible. Visualization is part of the psychology of the possible: if we believe something is possible, we can anticipate the obstacles and make it happen.

I have found that competitive benchmarking (measuring how competitors do things) is very useful in dismantling mindsets in businesses which believe that there is only one way to carry out a process.

WOULDN'T IT BE NICE IF . . . OR WIBNI

Without dissatisfaction, nothing would change. Creativity and visualization are driven by breaking out of old structures and patterns. WIBNI is a useful, fast technique for building up a picture of the future. Its companion is 'wouldn't it be awful if . . .' or WIBAI.

WOULDN'T IT BE FUNNY IF . . . OR WIBFI

Sometimes humour can get right to the heart of things. Try looking at the problem and use the WIBFI phrase to make some jokes about the problem. Often completing WIBFI can take you quite unexpectedly, right to the heart of the problem.

BUILDING A BRIDGE

Visualization is a mechanism for making journeys. It is also a creative means to fill the yawning, daunting gap between where we are, and where we want to be. We can use Post-its and the cartoon 'story-board' approach as a means of mapping a journey as a process of steps. We imagine each activity that must occur, and draw it on a Post-it, then construct a flow of Post-its between the problem as it is now, and how we would like it to be. The next step is to review all the Post-its, looking for gaps and duplication, then attempt to draw up a new concurrent flow in a shorter time period, using less resources.

> Visualization shouldn't be approached cold. A useful warm-up technique is the classic 'desert island' excursion exercise where individual members of the team brainstorm an item they might take on holiday, and subsequently the flora, fauna and indigenous inhabitants that might be found on a desert island.
>
> The session leader draws the features onto the island, then asks the team to imagine that they are on a ship wrecked offshore on a submerged reef, and they

must cross the island to activate a rescue-beacon. As they journey, they encounter the features (with a few extras thrown in) and imaginatively overcome them using the holiday items brainstormed at the outset.

DREAMING

Visualization is dreaming aloud. It can involve a return to a symbolic fairy-tale world of witches, giants, helping elves, wisemen, fools and other creatures, deliberately transforming all the elements and relationships of reality into symbolic characters of folk-tale. The archetypes of fairy stories can help us to explore the problem.

DIFFERENT PERSPECTIVES: SHOES AND ROLE-PLAY

Visualization uses metaphor, analogy and perspective. It is surprising how differently we can view a situation if we become someone inside it, or observe it from a different perspective. Practise 'walking a mile in someone else's shoes' – what does it feel like? what can you see? what's different?

If you are familiar with a character in a film or from history, for example, Richard III, Wellington, Leonardo da Vinci, Florence Nightingale, John F. Kennedy, Harpo Marx, imagine their view of the same problem. Ask yourself, what would they do in this situation? If you want to take no chances with a presentation, visualize the worst kind of audience and plan accordingly.

DRAWING PICTURES

Sometimes the act of drawing a picture of the problem as it is now, and the way we would like it to be can change our motivation, making it stronger.

Pictures are tremendously personal and sharing them makes people feel vulnerable. When you work with pictures, try to ask open questions about what's present and what's missing.

Do not tell the artist what their picture means; don't interpret the pictures. Encourage the artist to say what they mean in their own words, asking open questions at first – 'where are *you* in the picture?' 'who or what is missing?' 'why aren't they there?' – to help the artist play with the potential meaning of the drawing.

> I have been involved in several exercises where companies wanted to ask employees what they thought of the organization and its management, but were afraid to ask because of the fear of punishing feedback. I've found that asking employees to draw how they saw the organization through visualizing how they would describe it to an eight-year-old child, can be very productive. If the subject is approached with some humour and the promise of confidentiality, at least 90 per cent of employees respond with useful imagery which can be summarized in

small groups and distilled into clear messages for the directors. These messages are usefully depersonalized and yet in sufficient detail for action to follow, which addresses these messages without generating defensive, blocking behaviours on the part of the decision-makers.

Stage 5

SELECT THE SOLUTION

❖

At this stage, if you are lucky, you will be embarrassed at the rich-
ness of the options before you. It is a good idea to revisit the problem-statement and check that you have solved the problem as
specified, or whether you have just managed to go off on a little excursion
together.

1 TOSS A COIN

This is a very useful technique for finding out what you really want to do.
All you do is select the best options and toss a coin: heads for one solution, tails for the other. You find that you tend to keep tossing the coin
until the one you *really* want comes up.

2 SOLUTION-CRITERIA GENERATION

A central problem in selecting a solution is one of finding agreed terms or
language through which we can distinguish the solutions.

> A variation on the coin-tossing idea appeared in an episode of David Lynch's TV
> drama series *Twin Peaks*. An FBI agent set up a row of bottles, each representing
> a potential murder-suspect. He then blindly flung a stone at the row of bottles.
> The agent then pursued the suspect whose bottle was hit.

We may find it useful to extract the central idea out of this 'Tibetan' technique.

First, we decide to take each solution in turn, and compare it against all
the others, pretending to defend it against all others in order to generate

distinguishing characteristics which cumulatively might distinguish one solution from another. In other words, let's explore all the potential criteria which might apply in making our final choice. And second, rank all the criteria in terms of importance. We are now ready to consider weighting or attaching an estimated value to these criteria.

3 WEIGHTING SYSTEMS

Weighting systems are like an inverted pyramid of potential solutions.

❖   Go back to the problem-statement and generate a list of solution-criteria in terms of 'musts' and 'wants', essential elements and 'nice-to-haves'.

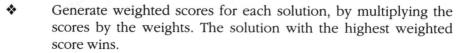

Fig S5.1 DECISION MAKING FITTERS

SOLUTIONS

SURVIVING SOLUTIONS

SOLUTION

❖   Review the solutions in terms of 'musts', discarding solutions without all the essential elements and retaining only those which satisfy the 'musts' criteria.

❖   Weight the 'wants' criteria in terms of usefulness on a scale of 1–10.

❖   Score the surviving solutions in terms of their relative performance within the 'wants' criteria.

❖   Generate weighted scores for each solution, by multiplying the scores by the weights. The solution with the highest weighted score wins.

Usually at this point, you realize that there is something wrong with the weighting of some of the 'wants' because it has produced a solution which you have no intention of implementing, or you discover that you have failed to include some important criteria.

SELECTING SOLUTIONS/DECISION-MAKING

(Filters, Musts, Wants, Weighting, Scoring and Arguing)

1   Generate solutions.
2   Identify *essential* solution-criteria = musts.
     Non-conformance means it is out of the process.
3   Develop *useful* solution-criteria = wants

or solution-differentiators. Weight the wants
in terms of usefulness (1–10).

4   Consider each solution in turn, scoring the wants.
5   Create weighted scores for every want by multiplying
       weights against scores, working through the surviving solutions.
6   Add the weighted scores, and select the highest score.

FIGURE S5.2 WEIGHTED SCORING OF ALTERNATIVES

SOLUTIONS

	WTG	A SCORE	A WT/SCORE	B SCORE	B WT/SCORE	C SCORE	C WT/SCORE
WANT	9	4	36	7	63	3	27
WANT	3	7	21	4	12	9	27
WANT	2	7	14	7	14	2	4
TOTAL		A	71	B	89	C	58

B 89   Highest
        Weighted Score
        = Solution

7   Disagree with the final solution, start again, or
8   Consider solution in terms of risks.

NOTES

❖   You may decide to generate your solution-criteria before you gen-
       erate solutions.

❖   Don't be surprised if you find you have chosen a solution you
       don't like the first time. It is part of the process.

❖   It should be fine to disagree with a solution, since it will lead to
       the inclusion of otherwise 'hidden' solution-criteria, or to expo-
       sure of biased weighting or scoring.

❖   You rarely have time, data, a complete range of choices, or the
       right people available to make a perfect decision.

❖   Try to involve the people who will implement the solution in the process of selection.

3 EASE AND EFFECT MATRIX

The Ease and Effect Matrix (EEM) is a way of prioritizing solutions by arranging them within a nine-box matrix of three columns by three rows.

FIGURE S5.3 THE EASE AND EFFECT MATRIX

	EASE High (3) V. Easy	Moderate (2)	Low (1) Difficult
EFFECT High (3) V. Effective	P1	P2	P3
Moderate (2)	P2	P3	P4
Low (1) Ineffective	P3	P4	P5

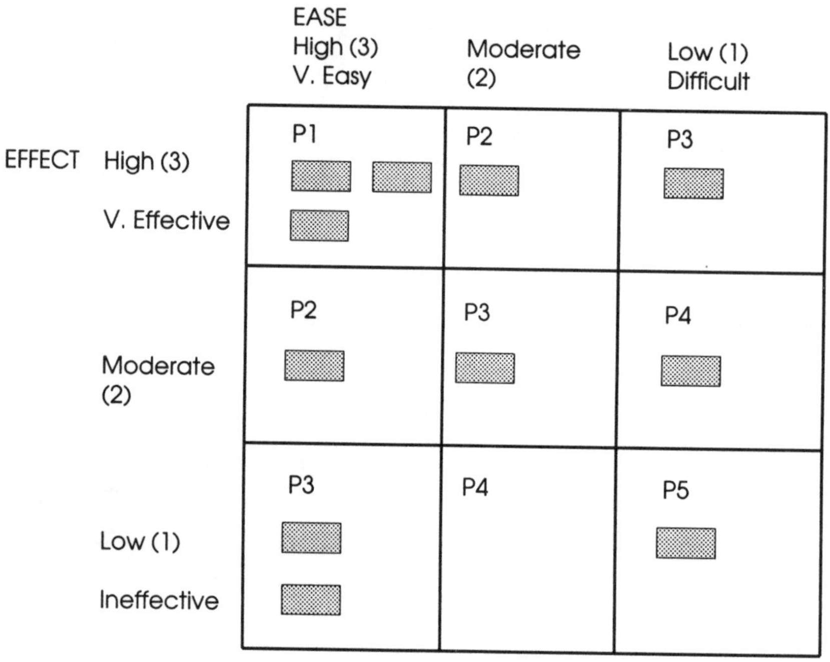

❖   Solutions are transferred onto Post-its (one per Post-it).

❖   Solution Post-its are scored using two different coloured pens as being either High (3), Moderate (2), or Low (1) in terms of *ease* of introduction and implementation (red pen), and *effect* if implemented (green).

❖   The EEM can be constructed so that the highest values are in the top left-hand box, and prioritized by location (P1 = highest priority, P2 = next highest priority, etc.).

❖   Once scored in terms of ease and effect, solution Post-its are located within the EEM.

4 AWAKISHI (REVERSED ISHIKAWA) OR SOLUTION AND EFFECT DIAGRAM

This is a reversal of the Ishikawa, putting the solution as the head of the fish at the left-hand side of the flipchart, using the same major *cause* labels as in the Ishikawa but as major *effects*, and examining the foreseeable impact which various solutions might have in different areas.

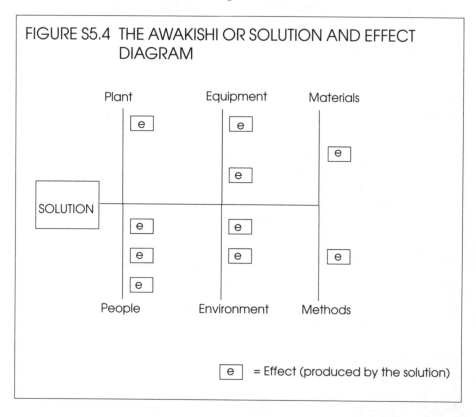

FIGURE S5.4 THE AWAKISHI OR SOLUTION AND EFFECT DIAGRAM

It is possible to 'weight' or prioritize the Awakishi, by colour-coding the effects which **must** be delivered. Awakishi allows you to test solutions in terms of what they must deliver.

5 ISHICOOPER (COMBINED PROBLEM CAUSES AND SOLUTION-EFFECTS DIAGRAM)

The Ishicooper integrates both the cause and effect fishbone with the solution and effect diagram. The technique requires that the initial cause and effect Ishikawa is given a solution 'fishhead' on the left, the spines made vertical and the resulting chart duplicated on as many sheets as there are solutions. Then the various solutions are tried out on the templates, and effects (e) predicted in terms of balancing existing causes

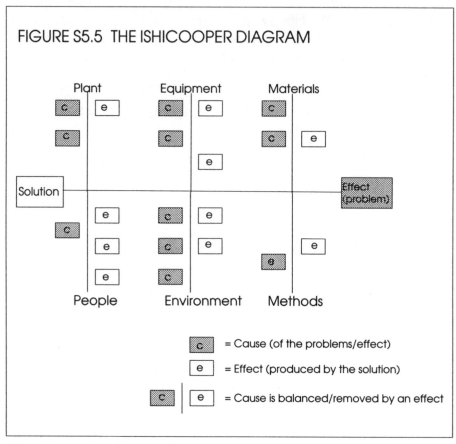

FIGURE S5.5 THE ISHICOOPER DIAGRAM

(c) and new disturbance effects.

Ishicooper is also useful for thinking yourself into the detail of implementation, and for developing 'what if?' scenarios.

6 PAIRS COMPARISON

Pairs comparison uses a matrix structure to compare a number of alternatives, selecting a final solution through ranking the alternatives on the basis of points allocated.

A simple approach is to draw up your matrix with your alternatives (in this case A–D) across both axes, blocking the resulting boxes where they intersect themselves with an 'X'. Agree your 'prefer to' side/axis of the matrix and system of allocating scores:

FIGURE S5.6 PAIRS COMPARISON MATRIX

4 points to allocate overall:

3 indicates a preference over another alternative, put 3 into that box, and allocate

1 to the complementary box (1 indicates that an alternative is less attractive).

2 suggests that you are unable to choose (put 2 in both boxes).

The horizontal axis is the 'prefer-to' axis.

	A	B	C	D
A	X	3 ●		
B	1 ●	X	▣ 2	
C			X	
D	D	▣		X
TOTALS				

Symbols indicate

● Prefers B to A

▣ Equal preference/can't distinguish between C and D.

The highest-scoring alternative wins (or provokes more discussion!)

Pairs comparison can also be used for a form of consensus-mapping, where you adopt a scoring system which reflects the number of voters preferring the proposition, with the converse box scoring the votes against. This can be useful as long as people don't start to vote tactically! Accordingly, you may need to conceal the scoring-matrix discreetly from direct view of the voting participants.

Stage 6

PLAN THE IMPLEMENTATION

'Plan to win, or plan to lose'

Planning to implement a solution requires a combination of sheer hard work and creativity. Failure to use imagination here, leaving detail to chance, will lead to chaos and lack of credibility in the future. Remember that our short stress-gaps tend to close down or reduce our ability to play with our imagination and develop all the fine, rich detail necessary to foresee all the potential risks and opportunities along the route.

It may be useful to build a model of the problem and think its metamorphosis through from initial to final state, in order to achieve a sufficient level of necessary detail.

It is often all very well to think things through, but few have the ability or will to challenge the plan, and ask themselves provocative questions about contingencies. Anticipating the future is one thing, making sure it happens is another.

My favourite example affecting life and death is the way Dr Steven Hughes of 2 PARA applied this type of imagination and daring to getting 2 PARA's medical capability ready for the Falklands War.

> Steven Hughes combined components of experience to make a potent contribution to planning to keep soldiers alive:
>
> First, he studied the experience of a Hercules transport aircraft becoming unserviceable and preventing the medical Landrover and trailer participating in an airborne exercise. Second, he saw how the Warren Point tragedy in Northern Ireland demonstrated a need for all soldiers to stabilize casualties where they fell. Finally, the experience of the Americans in Vietnam and more recently the Israeli Army showed the importance of replacing casualties' lost body-fluids quickly.
>
> Together, these observations led to essential medical equipment being carried by the medical team in their rucksacks; teaching everyone a mnemonic and associated casualty drill (ABE – airway, breathing and evacuation); issuing each soldier with a personal 1-lb. bag of fluid which they had to carry, and training one in ten paratroopers in how to administer fluid, intravenously.

1 KISS

KISS is a British Army mnemonic meaning Keep It Simple, Stupid. It doesn't mean to say that soldiers are stupid, but suggests that under stress, when a plan contains ambiguities or is difficult to understand, it will lead to misunderstandings.

KISS is the corollary of Murphy's Law: if it can go wrong, it will.

2 TACTICAL THINKING

Tactical Thinking (TT) is just a convenient way of packaging the obvious need to think into the implementation, foresee what could go wrong and deal with it.

TT is a four-stage process:

1   Identify all the problems you face
2   Put them into a logical sequence
3   Design actions which overcome the problems
4   Integrate the actions into an exhaustive plan-structure

3 OBJECTIFYING THE OBJECTIVE

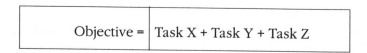

Objective =	Task X + Task Y + Task Z

A useful question to ask yourself as part of your visualization of the activities which together make up the complete plan is: How will I know when I have achieved my objective?

Then, produce a statement which begins: 'I'll know when I have achieved my objective, because X, Y and Z will have happened.'

It then becomes possible to break the objective down into sub-tasks which cumulatively deliver the objective. We can then introduce measures of performance linked to each task.

A variation on this approach is to ask another question: 'How will I be able to tell that this project is being run successfully?'. This can be answered through a list of all the cues or criteria which satisfy the following statement: 'I'll know the project is being run successfully because A, B and C will be happening.'

4 PLAN-GRID

A plan-grid is a simple technique for laying out a plan in terms of all the necessary actions in specific time-phases. It is an organization and methods approach to planning in two dimensions: individuals or team and time.

FIGURE S6.1 PLAN-GRID

PHASES		TEAM A	TEAM B	TEAM C
(Admin)	0			
	1			
	2			
	3			
	4			

If there are gaps in the plan-grid, this may mean that the processes involved require a pause or it may mean hidden waste in terms of utilization or employment of people. The implicit objective is to use the least resource in terms of people and time to complete a process.

Another advantage of the plan-grid is the way it allows the plan to be introduced to the team and understood by them.

When introducing the plan, as well as designing it, bear in mind Kipling's six Honest Serving-men: 'What and Why and When, How and Where and Who.'

What?	What are we doing?
Why?	Why must it be done?
When?	When must it happen?
How?	How will it be accomplished?
Where?	Where will it happen?
Who?	Who will do it?

5 MOT (MISSION, OBJECTIVES AND TASKS)

MOT is a hierarchical approach to structuring a project by working down from the top of a pyramid where the project 'mission' sits, through 'objectives' which together deliver the mission, and finally at the bottom: the 'tasks' which in turn, deliver the objectives.

FIGURE S6.2 THE MOT HEIRARCHY								
Mission								
Objective 1			Objective 2			Objective 3		
Task 1.1	Task 1.2	Task 1.3	Task 2.1	Task 2.2	Task 2.3	Task 3.1	Task 3.2	Task 3.3

Mission   The 'mission' statement must be short and sharp and express what the team will achieve in a positive manner. The statement should also include a timescale.

Objectives   'Objectives' specify the areas in which the team must make an impact. This is not specified in terms of jobs to do (tasks), but at an 'effect' level (overall results desired). A good way to arrive at a list of objectives is to ask the question: 'what do we want to be good at?'

Tasks   'Tasks' are specific, measurable and short-term. They are the 'jobs to do'.

Once you know the mission, identify all the key objectives which together, deliver the mission. With clear objectives, it becomes possible to specify the necessary tasks which in turn, deliver the mission.

❖   Once you know the necessary tasks, allocate timings, responsibilities, definition (how you will know that the task is complete) and personnel. Develop a task allocation sheet for each task.

❖   Each formal meeting must provide an update on tasks, any modifications, and new requirements.

❖   Only initiate and complete tasks which deliver the objectives, and in turn, the mission. Always ask yourself: 'should we be doing this activity?', 'does it help to deliver an objective?'

An often-overlooked aspect of project management is the problem of maintaining motivation and interest within a team operating over an extended period, sometimes remote from each other, or specializing in a particular area of research. In such a situation, it is a good idea to set up a display of the mission, objectives and tasks in the form of a MOT Wallchart timetable: with weekly columns throughout the project, with rows for the objectives and, in the resulting grid-boxes, Post-its representing the tasks. As tasks are completed, they can be scored through by those involved, at a meeting of the complete team. The key to the MOT wallchart is its accessibility, visibility and clarity.

MOT WALLCHART PROCESS

The MOT wallchart is the visual means to help you plan and manage your project successfully. To complete it take the following steps:

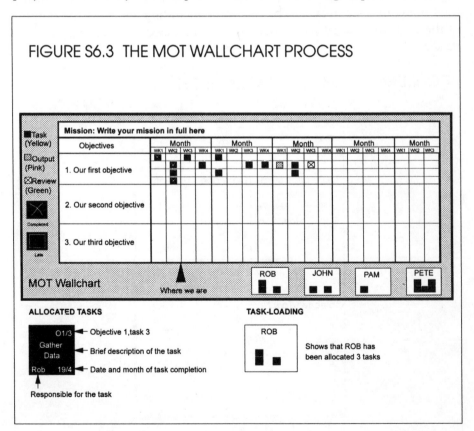

FIGURE S6.3 THE MOT WALLCHART PROCESS

1. Mission

Write the mission in full across the top of the chart; this provides a constant reminder to the team of why you started the project.

2. Objectives

Write the objectives in full down the left-hand margin.

3. Tasks

Brainstorm each objective in turn and determine all the tasks necessary to successfully complete that objective. Place each task onto a yellow Post-it with the following information on it:

O   Objective and task number
O   Brief description of task
O   Date and month of task completion
O   Name of person responsible for the task.

4. Task Allocation Sheet

Expand each task onto a full A4-sized task allocation sheet. This allows the full detail of each task to be recorded, including the expected outputs of the task (the things you expect to be able to see on completion of the task).

FIGURE S6.4 TASK ALLOCATION SHEET

Owner	Team:	
Date allocated	Date due	Sign-off:
Task Description:	Activities	
Objective/Task No:		
Outputs:		

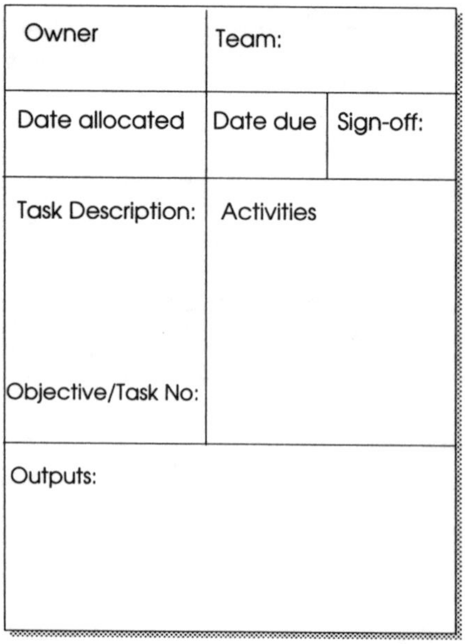

Task allocation sheets also force the team and individuals to confront the issue of what it is that they really want and to agree on how it is expressed. This is not a simple process. Individuals may agree to activities in outline and completely disagree in terms of detail. Work on defining the tasks now will prevent future, avoidable arguments.

5. Task Loading

At the bottom of the MOT wallchart, each team-member is given a separate task-loading sheet; copies of the task Post-its they are responsible for on the MOT wallchart, are attached. This provides an immediate idea of the amount of work each person is responsible for, the relative loading, and helps us to allocate future tasks more fairly.

6. Outputs

These are in the same format as tasks but placed on pink Post-its for ease of identification. These represent outputs such as presentation or reports.

7. Review

Review is expressed in the same format as task Post-its, but using green Post-its. These timetable reviews for managing the project over a long period and generally come at the end of defined stages within the project.

Once all the seven stages above have been defined, the project can begin to run in earnest. To show the progress achieved, the Post-its are 'crossed-off' when completed. This crossing-off and highlighting of tasks occurs at the end of each weekly meeting and must involve the whole team. The team decides if the task is complete and either crosses-off or highlights the Post-it border with a red flipchart pen if overdue. If tasks are delayed then it is for that person to inform the team and explain the reasons; finish dates can then be adjusted to reflect the delay. Finally, the Post-it arrow at the bottom of the MOT wallchart shows where the team are now, and simply progresses along the wallchart with time.

6 VISUALIZING THE WHOLE PROCESS

A good story has a beginning, a middle and an end. We can approach planning much like a storyteller by visualizing the plan in reverse: visualizing the finish, the middle, and finally the start.

By visualizing the end or the finish, we can construct a mindmap of the finish to build up a picture of just how the plan ends: what would tell us that we had succeeded? what would we be doing? how would we feel? what would people say to us? how would we be able to measure our success objectively in the eyes of our peers, our customers or our industry?

This visualization of the end can be in the form of a problem-map displaying the answers to these questions and providing a useful model to check the plan or middle against. We can sometimes summarize this finish-map of success-criteria into a mission or goal-statement.

We can then move on to visualizing the middle, the part often seen as the plan itself. We do this through the use of Post-its and creative silence, asking everyone to visualize every single activity that must occur to deliver the finish. We then go through phases of brainstorming and review, always looking forward to the finish to check that we are delivering a process that does what we want it to do, that tells us what will happen, how it will happen and when.

Finally, we do what is often forgotten in planning and visualize the start. What must be there at the start? What will we be doing, wearing, feeling, need to know, need to able to do? What must we understand and have designed processes to manage?

Ultimately, we can step back and ask ourselves whether we can say that we know. How it ends, how it runs, and how it starts.

7 REVERSAL/PLANNING BACKWARDS

Another useful technique is to reverse the flow of planning when you find that going forward is leading nowhere or you run out of ideas or find yourself blocked. Using visualization techniques, imagine that you are watching a video of the implementation plan being put into action, but try to play it backward so that you see each frame in reverse. Begin with the celebration party after the opening ceremony and reverse the 'video' frame by frame, noting all the activities on Post-its. Then integrate all the activities noted, into a *forward* flow.

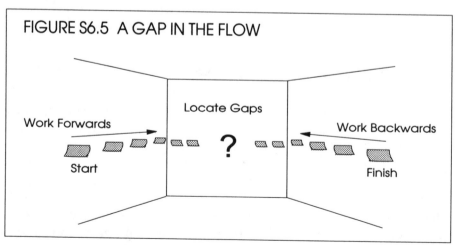

FIGURE S6.5 A GAP IN THE FLOW

8 PROCESS IMPROVEMENT

Once we have established a linear appreciation of all the steps or activities which together, cumulatively deliver the plan, we need to pause and consider. We may have listed all the activities but treated linearly, as discrete steps, they may just take too long. Figure S6.6 shows all the activities in the form of a wall of unstructured Post-its.

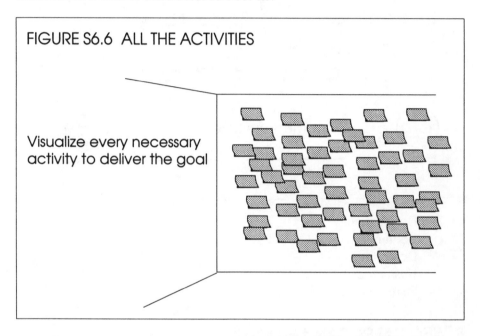

FIGURE S6.6 ALL THE ACTIVITIES

Visualize every necessary activity to deliver the goal

These are then sorted, gaps identified and filled, and redundant activities stripped out. We need to consider compressing the flow by identifying which tasks can be run concurrently (see Figure S6.7).

Once we have reduced *total time* through concurrency we can identify the bottleneck activities (those where activities converge, and once completed can lead to subsequent, diverging tasks). Once the bottlenecks are established, these can often be demolished by introducing extra resources at that point to widen the neck of the bottle.

When we have established the modified process, a pilot needs to be run eliminating waste in the following forms: hesitation, activity-duplication, confusion, and the amount of time in which resources are available and unused or underemployed.

In summary, establish the linear process sequence, then remove wasted time by reconfiguring into parallel flows of activity through concurrency. Then review the process, designing out all the unnecessary

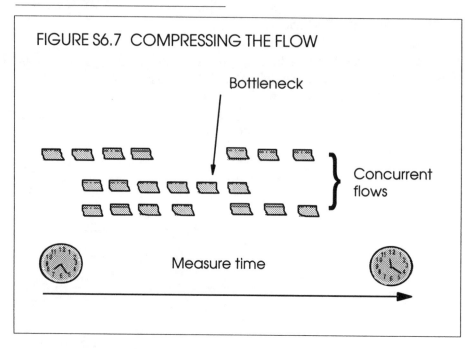

FIGURE S6.7 COMPRESSING THE FLOW

Bottleneck

Concurrent flows

Measure time

- O   Duplication
- O   Bottlenecks
- O   Dead-time
- O   Hesitation
- O   Spare material resource

8 WHO CARES, CAN AND WILL?

By asking yourself these three questions, you identify three influential groups of people, essential to the management of planned change:

Who cares?	Who will care whether we succeed with our plan? Whose life will change?
Who can?	Who is in a position to make it work?
Who will?	Who is committed to the implementation?

9 HOW/ HOW DIAGRAMS

This technique (the converse of Why/Why) tries to identify the necessary steps for implementing a solution. Having agreed your solution, you challenge by asking 'how?' and consequently develop a chain of activities. It is possible to link How/How to Why/Why, developing the How/How to overcome all the components of the Why/Why.

FIGURE S6.8 HOW/HOW DIAGRAM

How?	How?	How?	How?
'Introduce continuous improvement into organization'	Gain TMT commitment	Recruit Senior Mgrs from competitors where CI already exists	Compare performance with competition
	Overcome workforce resistance	Develop Middle-mgrs to introduce and support the process	Communicate 'agile/lean' manufacturing strategy
		Introduce team-level briefings	
	Introduce proactive problem-solving culture	Remove status demarcation	Single carpark/cafeteria
			Same holidays
		Measure and cost waste in system	Introduce meritocracy based on open values
		Fundamental review of manufacturing process	X-functional teamworking
		Audit internal supply-chain relationships	Encourage managers to work on the line
		Introduce problem-solving training for all, supported by trained managers	

Relate this How/How diagram back to the Stage 3: Why/Why diagram (see pp. 70–71) from which it came.

10 QUEST – QUICK ENVIRONMENTAL SCANNING TECHNIQUE

Quest is a technique for developing company strategy, finding and solving organizational problems. In outline it has six key stages:

1 'How far ahead do we need to plan?'
2 'What will be happening within our operational environment within that period?'
3 PEST: Political, Economic, Social and Technological trends and their likely impact on our environment
SWOT: Strengths, Weaknesses, Opportunities, Threats.
Bases of competition,
Critical Success Factors
4 'What do we have to do in order to remain successful?'
5 'What can we expect the company to do?'
6 'What can we do about it?' I call this establishing the 'Gap': the gap between what must be done and what would otherwise be done.

Stage 7

TEST/REHEARSE

'Train hard, fight easy'
Suvorov

In terms of the whole pantechnicon of implementation, testing individuals' knowledge and understanding and having the will to rehearse the process is the area requiring the greatest courage from a project-leader.

At the end of a briefing, it is insufficient to ask whether there are any questions. Everyone will tend to hold back from asking the key questions because they will assume that they are the only ones puzzled or confused by elements in the plan, and the question that needs to be asked will only expose them to the ridicule of everyone else who, of course, does understand.

Later on, closing their briefcases, in the corridor, by the coffee-machine, on the train or opening their car-boots to put their briefcases and laptops away, they will turn to each other and ask the question they really wanted to ask you: 'Now what did you mean, when you said...?'

The only solution is to test knowledge: by involving everyone in a rehearsal game, conducted as realistically as time permits.

During this rehearsal (which may be symbolic, like a game of chess), the plan and detail can be tested with the participation of the team, deliberately imagining themselves at various stages of the implementation:

O   What are they saying?
O   Who are they talking to?
O   How will they feel?
O   What happens next?

This imaginative rehearsal is similar to the preparation of athletes for a major event, where they actively visualize their own behaviour, from getting up on the morning of the event, through to receiving the award and making a speech of thanks.

Unfortunately, the only time plans are rehearsed exhaustively is when lives are at stake.

1 REHEARSAL

Rehearsal is a form of deep play. It allows our intellectual knowledge of the plan to become a deeper, shared understanding enabling creative response to unforeseen changes in circumstance.

The problem with rehearsal is the way it tends to be approached with closed eyes. It is as though by closing your vision down, you can somehow avoid potential risks and mistakes by trying not to see them, that is, if I cannot see them, they cannot hurt me. One of the commonplaces of observing the rehearsal of projects using models to walk through the process, is that the mistake made in rehearsal *always* appears again in the implementation. It just *won't* be all right on the night.

The key is to open your eyes in the rehearsal and use all your abilities to capture and observe the process in rehearsal, then apply all your process-improvement techniques to focus on simplification and waste.

2 ROLE-PLAY

As I suggested above, it can be very useful and insightful to think yourself into the role of either the subject you are about to interview, or into the role of a participant or customer. This can have startling results in terms of your ability to predict answers and behaviours to remain one step ahead.

Developing your empathic element can enable you to visualize the reaction of individuals to the changes you wish to implement, and disarm potential resistance.

3 WORST SCENARIO

Murphy's Law suggests 'If it can go wrong, it will'. We can plan for the worst case by visualizing that situation, its potential origins and collateral effects. The danger is that planning for the worst contingency can become an end in itself.

Stage 8

ACTION

❖

We have a powerful propensity to turn our backs on the problem-solving process, shut down our attention and wait for the finish. We feel that we have come so far that our plan will just happen, unleashing a whole stream of concurrent flows of activity which will carry us to the target.

This is premature. Everyone involved will need reassurance, since unexpected obstacles will appear. To this end, it is vital to organize a system of feedback which signals the end of successful stages and entry to new stages. Similarly, there is a need to report variations in the plan and take action.

We need to ensure that we have:

O Feedback
O Agreed reporting-points and mechanisms
O The ability to locate our progress in terms of the overall process
O Planned to celebrate our success.

The greatest danger of project-planning technique is the implicit assumption that as time passes, work is being done. 'It just ain't so!' It is important to inject emotion into the implementation. I have seen many situations where the planning has been in excellent detail and yet nothing seemed to happen. Specification isn't enough. Visible leadership is essential.

1 LIVE THE MESSAGE/ FILL THE GAP

To plan is insufficient. We have to live the message of the implementation. When we embark on implementing an idea, people feel the pull of the old way of doing things, a pull that means they have to say goodbye to the past, and experience a feeling of exposure as they move toward the future. Those involved in the implementation may understand the plan and their part in it, but will look to the leader of the implementation for behavioural cues that will give a keener impression of how serious and committed he or she is.

If we leave behavioural gaps or contradictions in our behaviours, we create ambiguity. In the absence of a clear message, we are inclined to fill the gaps with what we think the message is. If the ambiguity exists, then cynicism tends to fill it as people look at what you did, and discount what you said as a piece of camouflage.

Design a new behaviour that will underline and reinforce the message behind the implementation. If, like Julius Caesar, you can burn some bridges to show that you cannot retreat, then find them and burn them! If the project is to implement a teamworking culture, then get rid of your office and locate yourself with everyone else in the open-plan office downstairs; become a member of a subordinate's team.

2 GIVE FEEDBACK

Once we become aware that behaviour is the message and words are secondary, we need to be able to reinforce the message by giving feedback in a competent way without demotivating the subject of that feedback. If you witness negative behaviour, your failure to respond and remind the subject can lead to a degrading of their awareness of the symbolic meaning of their behaviour.

Let's take an everyday example. In Figure S8.1, the intervention has been made in the form of feedback to the subject, with the potential of either a new suggested behaviour emerging of putting litter in bins, or minor guilt feelings when the same old behaviour is performed!

Feedback is a two-way process, and should reflect a genuine willingness to work cooperatively. Some empathy with the position of the subject is necessary, in order to design and deliver the feedback without falling into a parent:child type of interaction which could trigger dismissive behaviours.

Feedback should be given:

- O   Directly: from me to you
- O   As a gift that can be used
- O   Reflecting the individual's needs
- O   Without value-judgement (no goods or bads)
- O   Specific to the incident, and if possible in time ('When I saw you/heard you ...').

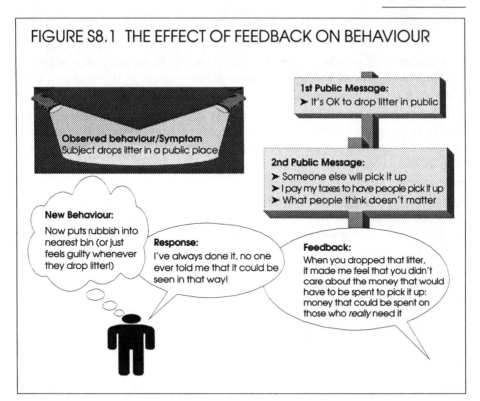

FIGURE S8.1 THE EFFECT OF FEEDBACK ON BEHAVIOUR

3 CELEBRATE

Some people think about implementing change or a project in the same way that they look after themselves. If they feel ill, they will put off going to the doctor in the hope that the pain will go away; apply this attitude to a project and the project will eventually die. Celebration demonstrates our commitment to the project, and develops our sense of progress and belief in approaching the final goal.

> I remember a systems implementation within a service company where, once the system was up and running, a few people from the cross-functional team who had made strong friendships had an unofficial drink in a pub to mark the finish. However, most team members had other commitments back in their own part of the business or didn't know about the get-together because it was unofficial, and low-key. The cross-functional team never met again as a body. There were some personal issues about relationships during the project that had not been addressed, and these remained below the surface. Six months later, I returned to the company and found that these personal issues were still nagging in the backs of people's minds affecting their work with the people concerned. This bad feeling was affecting their willingness to get involved in future projects. When I investigated this further, I discovered that because we had never said goodbye to the project, people were still carrying the issues and could not symbolically

discard them to move on. From that point on, I made sure that if I could influence the decision, we would celebrate success.

A celebration needs to be a social occasion, reinforcing our sense of community. It needs to include a review of the success so far, and a look forward into the next oncoming stage where minor or even major issues can be raised and addressed. Examples of celebration can be diverse: from a Lego model reflecting progress on the actual site, to a temperature-gauge, or symbolic jigsaw where the completed jigsaw means the project is complete. Needless to say, the final celebration must be the most memorable!

The key message to remember is to make people feel good about what they are doing, especially if it is new and requires abandoning the past. If they can associate good feelings and success with doing new things, they are more likely to be successful and positive in future implementations.

PART IV

SOME
CONCLUSIONS

❖

CONCLUSIONS

❖

The most interesting aspect of problem-solving is why people fail to use a process either on their own problems or to facilitate teams in solving problems. The key obstacle is the perceived *reality* of the situation, in other words, the Catch-22 circular logic that says: 'The reason we don't use problem-solving techniques or process to solve problems is because that isn't the way work is done around here.'

I saw this most clearly in an industrial consultancy where a senior partner demanded that fishbone diagrams were removed from display areas where customers could see them. When he was asked to explain his thinking, he said that these diagrams had to be removed because they gave the customer the impression that 'we don't get things right first time', in other words: 'we make mistakes'. He was not a stupid man, and perhaps he understood the culture of the customer-base best. The sad fact is that he never set them up somewhere else in the office.

Problem-solving is a cultural issue and it revolves around the issue of *what constitutes work and who has the power to define it* for the organization and the individual.

Books on measurement systems and organizational anthropology often point out how people are constrained to behave in ways that do not help the business. A common element in many large organizations is the conspicuous consumption of time: where individuals arrive early, leave late, and do so in a way that ensures that you notice it. It is pointless to dismiss this behaviour as plain silly: people wouldn't do it unless they were receiving the cues that said this behaviour is valid and that it constitutes work.

Unless individuals have actually managed to save their own lives through applying what is essentially a complete problem-solving drill-sequence, they may tend to stay at the practitioner level of the Coyote, or the Competitor. Understanding problem-solving is not the same as practice, and again this leads us to the discussion about whether we see problem-solving as an arcane art-form or as a tool. Too many well-educated senior managers recognize the problem-solving process, but maintain this knowledge purely as part of their intellectual furniture.

The failure to deploy problem-solving processes is probably due to our assumptions about what is acceptable or appropriate behaviour in the social aspect of the work-situation. I'd like to draw an analogy with the ambiguous but very interesting Milgram (1974) Experiment.

Essentially, Professor Milgram created what appeared to be a learning laboratory. Individuals were paid to take part in administering a learning experiment setting learning tasks for what they were told was a 'student' and punishing them with electric shocks when they made mistakes. As the experiment progressed, the voltage would rise. The legitimacy of the procedure was supported by an authority-figure who pretended to be the experimenter. The idea was to see just how far the subject would go in punishing the 'student' with increasingly severe penalties. What was surprising was the high level of conformance by participating individuals to the point of continuing to punish the 'student' even when they were apparently begging for mercy.

Whereas Milgram relates his experiment to atrocity research, it is arguable that perhaps this tells us more about how the individuals felt about students!

The relevance of Milgram's experiment to problem-solving lies in the link with social behaviour and the cues which the ambient work environment offers. These cues for social obedience, in the form of body language, the semiotics of architecture, clothing, and perceived hierarchy discourage the application of problem-solving. When we apply a problem-solving process, we can find ourselves challenging all this. No wonder courage is needed not just to deal with what is present in the situation, but also with what we *think* is present.

We need the courage that allows us to detach ourselves and introduce play into our work. That it is *play*, is what makes it so frightening for us all. To introduce creative techniques into the work situation is to offer the disturbing possibility that everything is flexible, especially reality and social relationships, and that a host of mindsets or contingent theories of political and social cause-and-effect by which we view the world and run our businesses are no more than convenient theories.

As I said in Part II, we need to desensitize ourselves from such social cues and sensitize ourselves to new opportunities, because if we don't practise the approach we tend to forget it.

Our desensitization to some social cues is necessary, because sometimes we will get it wrong: we will apply techniques which subsequently turn out to be inappropriate and we need the courage to look silly. But I always take as my problem-solving practitioner moral: better to look silly than to fail; and if we do fail, better a sin of commission than omission.

If we look forward to where creative thinking appears to be current and the basis of change, we see the opportunity to apply the problem-solving process to confront the organizational mindset and completely redesign organizations out of all former recognition. This profound opportunity if it is truly open, allows us to redesign who does the work, how it is done and even what constitutes work itself. It is not surprising that success is relatively rare. After all, to confront the organizational mindset means that the chief executive has to have the flexibility and the wit to look in the mirror and refuse, like Groucho Marx, to join any club that would have someone like himself in it! It is a bit like getting to the top of the organization and realizing that if you've arrived there something must be wrong. As John Harvey-Jones suggested, you tend to know when the business has changed because you're no longer in it!

A relatively recent development is the arrival of computer-based technology to support group problem-solving across electronic networks or linked PCs within organizations and in teams in the form of Groupware. Groupware links individuals, and data through a protocol mirroring the problem-solving process to make decisions and help individuals to work together constructively. This can be either in the form of a session involving everyone working across the system simultaneously, working through the necessary steps, with summaries, and decisions at key stages through electronic voting; or over a longer period, enabling people with discontinuous schedules to participate through the phases. One can begin to see the potential for a unified organizational culture that does not require physical presence for participation, but which depends on individuals no longer 'owning' their own data and ideas, and willing to cast them into the organizational 'thinking-pot' through the Groupware system. What I do feel continues to hold Groupware back is the lack of excitement and the social opportunity that working together brings to creativity in groups. The Groupware processes mirror Nominal Group techniques electronically and provide the opportunity to involve a bigger organization in the thinking process. However, like distance learning, there is nothing quite like having an excellent facilitator in the room guiding everyone through a shared and explicit process.

If you have approached this book sensibly, you will have completed your Problem-Solving Styles Proforma at the outset and then prioritized your study of the eight areas of the PSP wheel accordingly. The true test will come when you sketch your PSP wheel onto your notepad before a meeting and ask questions that drive the meeting around as much of the process as is necessary to solve a problem.

FIGURE IV.1 THE PROBLEM-SOLVING PROCESS WHEEL

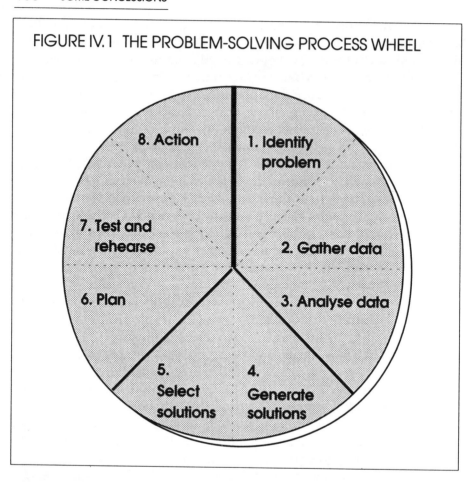

The important thing to remember is that there is nothing wrong with solving problems like the Coyote or the Competitor: just be honest with yourself when you are doing it, and make sure that it was a conscious choice.

RECOMMENDED READING

Ackoff, R.L. (1978) *The Art of Problem-Solving*; New York: Wiley.

Ackoff's willingness to apply experimental technique to the work of consulting pays some interesting dividends, especially where he demonstrates how a client's closed perception of correctness and undisclosed criteria of what constitutes a solution can disable a creative idea, because it is just not recognizable as a solution. Another admirable feature of his work is the way he includes sufficient detail in his examples for his conclusions to be rather ambiguous. We are all indebted to him for his 'fishy story' and his wicked sense of humour.

Adams, J.L. (1979) *Conceptual Blockbusting – A Guide to Better Ideas*; New York: Norton.
Adams, J.L. (1988) *The Care and Feeding of Ideas*; Harmondsworth: Penguin.

A pleasant trip through the issues of creativity, good analogies and explanation. A trend and agenda-setter in this area.

Aitkenhead, A.M. and Slack, J.M. (1985) *Issues in Cognitive Modelling*; London: Open University: Lawrence Erlbaum.

As the title suggests, goes deeply into the issue of how the mind appears to work, discussing perceptual organization, problem-solving as information-processing, and analogical problem-solving. A bit deep.

Arthur, M. (1985) *Above All, Courage – The Falklands Frontline: First-Hand Accounts*; London: Sidgwick & Jackson.

I learned about Steven Hughes' contribution to saving lives from this book. A really good book, with lots of emotion and accounts in individuals' own words delivering hard-edged gems of lessons to be learned from people who did their problem-solving under the toughest conditions.

Bales, R.F. and Strodtbeck, F.L. (1951) 'Phases in Group Problem-Solving', *Journal of Abnormal Social Psychology*. pp. 46, 485–495.

Bales' ideas probably influenced many people like Belbin, and Margerison and McCann, with their models of individual predispositions to certain team roles. Particularly striking is his premise that group behaviour is analogous to individual behaviour: that individuals deploy a repertoire based on previous success, and that task-oriented groups progress through definite phases of behaviour.

de Bono, E. (1967) *The Use of Lateral Thinking*; Harmondsworth: Pelican
de Bono, E. (1978) *Teaching Thinking*; Harmondsworth: Penguin.
de Bono, E. (1981) *The Mechanism of Mind*; Harmondsworth: Pelican
de Bono, E. (1982) *de Bono's Thinking Course*; London: BBC.

I have been rather cruel in ignoring most of de Bono's output here, but like most profound thinkers he has a tendency to say the same thing many times, and to invent techniques which already exist. His best work includes the above titles. *The Mechanism of Mind* is brilliant and well worth reading to develop sound mental models of problem-solving. His greatest weakness lies in ignoring the opportunity to enhance creativity and learning through group dynamics. In *Teaching Thinking*, he couldn't have been more wrong when he said: 'There is not much more you can do with a simple process except to state it' (de Bono, 1978, p. 117).

Bruner, J.S. (1960) *Towards a Theory of Instruction*; Cambridge, Massachusetts: Harvard University Press.

Bruner's theory of functional fixedness should feature in any serious discussion of the obstacles to effective problem-solving.

Buzan, T. (1982) *Use Your Head*; London: BBC/Ariel Books.

Buzan has taken what is known about how the mind organizes itself, and applied in a workable technique to aid recall and note-making.

Carter, R., Martin, J., Mayblin, B. and Munday, M. (1984) *Systems, Management and Change*; London: Open University: Harper & Row.

The most readable introduction to systems thinking yet.

Dupuy, T.N. (1977) *A Genius for War – The German Army and General Staff 1807–1945*; London: Prentice-Hall.

Unless you are a military historian, this may not be your book. However, some interesting points are made about the German/Prussian institution-alization of intellectual excellence in its staff-corps. In terms of problem-solving, this book is the source of the term 'operational' as an intermediate level between strategic and tactical, and, most interesting of all, the tactical doctrine which would define a task as denying the ground to the enemy, not holding it, freeing a subordinate to choose and interpret the task for themselves. Like some modern management studies on indus-trial performance, the measurement of fighting-ability on the battlefield seem questionable.

Goldratt, E.M. and Cox, J. (1989) *The Goal*; Aldershot: Gower.

An excellent book, written in the form of a novel. It introduces the idea of understanding work as a process, and the idea of tracking the process to find the bottlenecks that constrain just how fast it can go.

Gordon, W.J.J. (1961) *Synectics – The Development of Creative Capacity*; New York: Harper & Row.

One of the key books for any student interested in the management of group dynamics in problem-solving.

Hammer, M. and Champy, J. (1993) *Reengineering The Corporation – A Manifesto for Business Revolution*; London: Nicholas Brealey.

I like this book's iconoclasm; it is read by many but falls short of Peters' Biblical proportions and injunctions. The authors fail to understand the dangers of purchasing technologies as an end in themselves. Everything we know about escaping from mindsets can be applied legitimately to organizations and perhaps they are wise in just raising the curtain a little to give us a glimpse of what is possible. Weakest on just how the alterna-tive vision is developed in the existing business.

Henry, J. (1991) *Creative Management*; London: Sage.

An interesting compendium of the issues of creative management and their applications.

Holt, J. (1965) *How Children Fail*; Harmondsworth: Penguin.

I must admit to being heavily influenced by Holt's producer:thinker model of learning (routine learning as opposed to learning to understand), and by his insistence on the importance of teaching the right methods to get the right answers.

Isenberg, D.J. (1984) 'How Senior Managers Think', *Harvard Business Review*, Nov/Dec, pp. 81–90.

Isenberg, D.J. (1986) 'The Structure and Process of Understanding – Implications for Managerial Action', in *The Thinking Organisation – The Dynamics of Social Cognition*, ed. by Sims Jr, H.P. and Gioia, D.A. & Associates; New York: Jossey Bass, pp. 239–261.

Isenberg's work on how managers think mirrors and supports much of what has already been said in other forms especially in defining the goals for improving management thinking along lines parallel to Bruner.

Kepner, C.H. and Tregoe, B.B. (1981) *The New Rational Manager*, Princeton, New Jersey: Princeton Research Press.

The classic text. Although tedious and repetitious like most American approaches to problem-solving it is detailed and comprehensive. One day the authors will realize that their three problem-solving wheels are a variation on a single theme and that case-studies just teach you how to solve that particular *class* of problem and not how to approach solving *all* problems.

Majaro, S. (1988) *The Creative Gap – Managing Ideas for Profit*, Harlow: Longman.

An interesting and comprehensive text, with examples from consultancy. Supported by useful proformas for company creativity initiatives.

Masaaki, Imai (1986) *Kaizen – The Key to Japan's Competitive Success*, New York: McGraw-Hill.

Lifts the lid on the thinking behind what was to become called 'lean manufacturing'. A seminal text with many examples of problem-solving applications within Japanese industry.

Mayon-White, B. (1986) *Planning and Managing Change*, London: Harper.

A stimulating collection of articles serving to challenge mindsets about how work is approached and organized.

Milgram, S. (1974) *Obedience to Authority*, London: Tavistock.

A classic text in social psychology much marred by references to the then-topical Vietnam War: ultimately fails to resolve the enigma of just what the experiments proved.

McLeish, J., Matheson, W. and Park, J. (1973) *The Psychology of The Learning Group*, London: Hutchinson.

A seminal text. I found my copy in a bin outside a library, it started me off on this route and promoted my interest in the use of problem-solving as a vehicle to develop individual learning through working in teams.

Morgan, G. (1993) *Imaginization – The Art of Creative Management*, California: Sage.

A very useful display of just how far and how useful creative metaphor and its allies, imagination and visualization can be working together.

Musashi, M. (1984) *A Book of Five Rings*, London: Flamingo.

The simplicity of this book cuts like a samurai sword. Musashi's dicta have power beyond his time to influence us now. You will want to take up Kendo.

Prince, G.M. (1970) *The Practice of Creativity*, New York: Harper & Row.

Like Gordon's, another book that all researchers will want to read in order to understand synectics.

Rhinehart, L. (1989) *The Diceman*, London: Grafton.

A silly but entertaining book that takes the idea of living through taking random choices by rolling a dice. Completely misses the point that the choices were not themselves randomly generated.

Rickards, T. (1988) *Creativity at Work*, Aldershot: Gower.

Rickards' work is easy to absorb; its attractive format encourages creative dipping and playing with the techniques.

VanGundy Jr., A.B. (1988) *Techniques of Structure Problem Solving*, New York: Van Nostrand Reinhold.

A heavy volume, closely-printed and full of detail. It documents just about everything that anybody has packaged as a problem-solving process, and shows just how tedious creativity could be without a sense of humour.

Weisberg, R.W. (1986) *Creativity, Genius and Other Myths*, New York: Freeman.

Weisberg breaks away from the pack of traditional creativitists who continue to broadcast the idea of group creativity being better than individual, in spite of the research to the contrary. Mounts a very strong attack on what he calls the myths of creativity and details many of the contradictions virtually all authors ignore.

Womack, J.P., Jones, D.T. and Roos, D. (1990) *The Machine That Changed The World*, New York: Rawson.

The mindset-buster of the decade that attempts to explain the West's weakness in automotive manufacture by showing just how differently the Japanese approach the business of designing, making and managing. Introduced the idea of Lean Production as a way of life, and shows how an aesthetic perception of waste allied to an awareness of strategic dependence on imported raw materials, plus MITI's injunction to reduce waste in their manufacturing processes after the 1973 oil-crisis led to a different perspective on how to manufacture.

Zuboff, S. (1988) *In the Age of the Smart Machine – The Future of Work and Power*, Oxford: Heinemann.

A fascinating book. An essay that clearly got out of control. Zuboff has taken McLuhan's dictum of the medium being its own message and through her study of the impact of IT on businesses, developed her own concept of 'informating': the *new* work of interpreting the data that new systems provide.

INDEX

T his index shows pages for figures and tables in italics, and the numbers in bold indicate chapters covering subjects.

Best Practice Benchmarking

Sylvia Codling

Benchmarking is potentially the most powerful weapon in the corporate armoury. It's the technique that enabled Cummins Engine Company to slash delivery time from eight months to eight weeks, Lucas to reduce the number of shopfloor grades at one of its sites from seventeen to four and British Rail to cut cleaning time for a 660-seat train to just eight minutes. In other companies order processing time has been brought down from weeks to days, engineering drawings output doubled and inventory cut by two-thirds.

And yet, in spite of the articles, the seminars and the conferences, managers continue to ask "What is benchmarking?" and "How do we do it?" The purpose of this book is to answer those questions. Through a series of case histories and references it shares the experience and knowledge acquired by benchmarking companies across a wide range of industries. Above all, it provides a detailed step-by-step guide to the entire process, including a complete set of planning worksheets.

Case studies include: Siemens Plessey, Volkswagen, British Rail, Lucas Industries, Shell, Rover and Hewlett Packard.

Benchmarking is a flexible discipline that has become a way of life in some of the world's most successful organizations. Learning from the best can help your own company to become a world leader in those areas that are critical to its performance. In so doing you will achieve an enduring competitive edge.

1995   168 pages   0 566 07591 1

Gower

50 Essential Management Techniques

Michael Ward

Are you familiar with the concept of product life cycle? Of course you are! Does the prospect of a SWOT analysis bring you out in a cold sweat? Probably not. But what about the Johari Window? Or Zipf's Law?

Michael Ward's new book brings together a formidable array of tools designed to improve managerial performance. For each entry he introduces the technique in question, explains how it works, then goes on to show, with the aid of an entertaining case study, how it can be used to solve an actual problem. The 50 techniques, including some never before published, are grouped into eleven subject areas, ranging from strategy to learning.

For managers in every type of organization and at any level, as well as for students and consultants, *50 Essential Management Techniques* is likely to become an indispensable source.

Summary of Contents

Part I Managing Strategy • Part II Managing Marketing • Part III Managing Pricing • Part IV Managing Finance • Part V Managing Operations • Part VI Managing Decisions • Part VII Managing Numbers • Part VIII Managing People • Part IX Managing Learning • Part X Managing Yourself • Part XI Managing Change.

1995   232 pages   0 566 07532 6

Gower

The Goal

Beating the Competition
Second Edition

Eliyahu M Goldratt and Jeff Cox

Written in a fast-paced thriller style, *The Goal* is the gripping novel which is transforming management thinking throughout the Western world.

Alex Rogo is a harried plant manager working ever more desperately to try to improve performance. His factory is rapidly heading for disaster. So is his marriage. He has ninety days to save his plant – or it will be closed by corporate HQ, with hundreds of job losses. It takes a chance meeting with a colleague from student days – Jonah – to help him break out of conventional ways of thinking to see what needs to be done.

The story of Alex's fight to save his plant is more than compulsive reading. It contains a serious message for all managers in industry and explains the ideas which underlie the Theory of Constraints (TOC) developed by Eli Goldratt – the author described by Fortune as 'a guru to industry' and by Businessweek as a 'genius'.

As a result of the phenomenal and continuing success of *The Goal*, there has been growing demand for a follow-up. Eliyahu Goldratt has now written ten further chapters which continues the story of Alex Rogo as he makes the transition from Plant Manager to Divisional Manager. Having achieved the turnround of his plant, Alex now attempts to apply all that Jonah has taught him, not to crisis management, but to ongoing improvement.

These new chapters reinforce the thinking process utilised in the first edition of *The Goal* and apply them to a wider management context with the aim of stimulating readers into using the technique in their own environment.

1993   352 pages   0 566 07417 6 Hardback   0 566 07418 4 Paperback

Gower

It's Not Luck

Eliyahu M Goldratt

Alex Rogo has had a great year, he was promoted to executive vice-president of UniCo with the responsibility for three recently acquired companies. His team of former and new associates is in place and the future looks secure and exciting. But then there is a shift of policy at the board level. Cash is needed and Alex's companies are to be put on the block. Alex faces a cruel dilemma. If he successfully completes the turnaround of his companies, they can be sold for the maximum return, but if he fails, the companies will be closed down. Either way, Alex and his team will be out of a job. It looks like a lose-lose situation. And as if he doesn't have enough to deal with, his two children have become teenagers!

As Alex grapples with problems at work and at home, we begin to understand the full scope of Eli Goldratt's powerful techniques, first presented in *The Goal*, the million copy best-seller that has already transformed management thinking throughout the Western world. *It's Not Luck* reveals more of the Thinking Processes, and moves beyond *The Goal* by showing how to apply them on a comprehensive scale.

This book will challenge you to change the way you think and prove to you that it's not luck that makes startling improvements achievable in your life.

1994   288 pages   0 566 07637 3

Gower

Problem Solving in Groups
Second Edition

Mike Robson

Modern scientific research has demonstrated that groups are likely to solve problems more effectively than individuals. As most of us knew already, two heads (or more) are better than one. In organizations it makes sense to harness the power of the group both to deal with problems already identified and to generate ideas for enhancing effectiveness by reducing costs, increasing productivity and the like.

In this revised and updated edition of his successful book, Mike Robson first introduces the concepts and methods involved. Then, after setting out the advantages of the group approach, he examines in detail each of the eight key problem solving techniques. The final part of the book explains how to present proposed solutions, how to evaluate results and how to ensure that the group process runs smoothly.

With its practical tone, its down-to-earth style and lively visuals, this is a book that will appeal strongly to managers and trainers looking for ways of improving their organization's and their department's performance.

Contents

Part I: Introduction • The benefits of group problem solving • Problem-solving groups • Part II: Problem-Solving Techniques • The problem-solving process • Brainstorming • Defining problems clearly • Analysing problems • Collecting data • Interpreting data • Finding solutions • Cost-benefit analysis • Part III: Following Through • Presenting solutions • Working together • Dealing with problems in the group • Index.

1993   176 pages   0 566 07414 1 Hardback   0 566 07415 X Paperback

Gower

Structured Problem Solving
A PARSEC Guide

Graham W Parker

Problems represent the difference between where we are now and where we want to be – obstacles in the journey to our goals. They erode our ability to compete, they prevent our success and they undermine our morale. Successful organizations, though, regard a problem as an opportunity for improvement – for learning a lesson that can be put to profitable use. In such organizations identifying and eliminating problems has become a way of life.

This book provides a systematic approach to solving business problems, designed to maximize the likelihood of finding the optimum solution in each case. Part I outlines the process involved. Part II describes and illustrates no fewer than 33 problem-solving "tools" and includes a grid that enables their respective uses and merits to be compared at a glance. Managers and other professionals will find this new PARSEC Guide a powerful aid to more effective performance.

Contents

Figures • Preface • Abbreviations • Problems, obstacles and opportunities for improvement • Systematic problem solving • Tools and the tools grid • Recognizing the problem • Defining the problem • Selecting the problems to work on • Characterizing the problem • Development and selection of solutions • Planning and implementation • Implementing full control • Creativity and teamwork • Bibliography • Glossary of tools.

1995   160 pages   0 566 07566 0

Gower